THE POWER TO COMMUNICATE
SECOND EDITION

The Power to Communicate
Gender Differences as Barriers
Second Edition

Deborah Borisoff
Lisa Merrill

WAVELAND

PRESS, INC.

Prospect Heights, Illinois

For information about this book, write or call:

Waveland Press, Inc.
P.O. Box 400
Prospect Heights, Illinois 60070
(708) 634-0081

Contents

Preface

This book addresses two essential issues that are often missing from works that deal with communication. First, it examines the impact of the stereotyped gender differences that are so powerful a force in male and female development, communication, and in male and female professional contexts.

Second, this book includes strategies and techniques that may be helpful to both women and men in dealing with persistent traditional attitudes and in attempting to break from them.

Following Chapters I, II, III and IV, we have provided numerous activities and exercises that can be used in a variety of instructional and training situations. These activities have been created to target both communication skills, such as listening ability and conflict resolution, and settings, such as one-to-one dyads, small group situations, and public communication contexts.

Introduction

Defining the Gender Gap
The Need for Cooperation in
a Technological Age.

Nearly every decade in American culture can be singled out for special achievements or strides. The last two decades are no exception—especially in the area of accomplishments by women. During the initial years of this period, for the first time a woman was appointed to the Supreme Court, served as a member of a space mission, and was nominated as a Vice-Presidential candidate for a major American party. These breakthroughs for women indicate that today America is in the throes of a social revolution in which individuals are expanding upon the traditional expectations for their sex.

While advancements in the area of technology can be clearly measured, social changes are more difficult to assess, often requiring the distance of decades—in some instances, centuries.

Within the past two decades, one social issue that has emerged in the forefront of American culture is the gender gap. Because increasing numbers of women are pursuing careers and because many men are sharing more equally the responsibilities of the home, both sexes are now required to demonstrate communicative behavior that previously belonged to the repertoire of the opposite sex. This change in behavior is easier to consider intellectually than it is to achieve because it is no small task to break from our prescribed cultural upbringing. Telling a woman she must be aggressive to succeed in business when she has been raised to be a polite young lady is just as difficult as instructing a man to share equally in the household chores when he was raised by a full-time homemaker who attended to his every need. In both cases, breaking from tradition is required, and this is very hard to do.

Both because the urge to maintain the *status quo* is powerful among many segments of our population, and because many individuals are now striving for opportunities long denied them, it is necessary to understand the consequences of bridging the communication gender gap. To do so, it is necessary to gain an insight into the communicative behavior that is part of the male and female experience in American society. This is exactly what researchers have endeavored to accomplish in recent years.

Research findings have been compiled in a variety of areas that deal with communication differences between the sexes. Physiological and psychological development has been of steady interest and concern to social scientists. Sociological research has increasingly emerged on the role of men and women in society and on their attitudes toward relationships, work, money and sex. The implications of language use as it affects the development and perceived roles of young children in society has been one focus of linguists. Nonverbal behavior as a powerful communication force continues to attract the interest of scholars from a variety of academic disciplines.

The research in the areas of psychology, sociology and linguistics demonstrates that the difference in communication styles between women and men in American culture is very real indeed. Although differences in the behaviors expected of either sex have always existed in our society, the explanations for interpretations of these disparities have changed over time.

For example, a century ago, it was argued that women were ill-suited physiologically to intellectual endeavors and that higher education would adversely affect them. At the present time, few would argue that women are biologically unfit for these pursuits. This example demonstrates a shift in perspective supporting the contention that biological factors alone do not determine behavior. Therefore, the distinctions between male and female behavior identified in this text are referred to as gender rather than sex differences because they are socially constructed and not innate.

In this book, we will consider these existing communication differences, implied sexual stereotypes and the barriers these stereotypes impose on men and women. We will also explore successful professional communication strategies and future implications of men and women working more closely together. By examining the differences in communication styles we hope to provide a means to enrich and expand the communication behavior of both men and women. The rewards of such change may accrue not only in the professional arena but also in the area of interpersonal relationships. Both sexes stand to benefit by such an understanding. Both will benefit from a more equal participation in the communication process.

chapter **1**

The Stereotype

Fiction or Fact

"Sir, a woman's preaching is like a dog's walking on his hind legs. It is not done well, but you are surprised to find it done at all."

—Samuel Johnson

"Why—do they shut Me out of Heaven
Did I sing—too loud?"

—Emily Dickinson

Public speaking is an assertive act. "Speech" and "voice" are frequently used as metaphors for power. It is in the act of giving voice to one's thoughts and feelings that a speaker has the potential to affect the thoughts and behavior of others.

Throughout much of recorded history, women have been forbidden to or actively discouraged from exercising their power of speech in public settings. Female silence has been equated with modesty, obedience, and womanly virtue (Keohane, 1981). Social and religious injunctions against women communicators have abounded. In the *New Testament*, Saint Paul instructed men to "Let a woman learn in silence with all submissiveness." He said, "I permit no woman to teach or to have authority over men; she is to keep silent." (I Timothy 2:9-15).

The authors of this text are both teachers; readers of this text presumably are enlightened twentieth century women and men, yet all of us have been influenced by what historically has been considered *appropriate* communicative behavior for our respective sexes. In this chapter, we discuss the stereotypical expectations placed upon speakers of both sexes, some of the sanctions anticipated and endured by those who violate the expectations, and the process by which gender-based stereotypes have been internalized.

I. Feminine Stereotypes

Background

In the 1650s, Anne Hutchinson was exiled from the Massachusetts Bay Colony because she attempted to have a voice in religious affairs. Hutchinson's "crime" was that she led meetings, called "conversations," in her home for groups of sixty or more people who came to listen to her theories about Christ. Her eloquent demeanor infuriated her accusers. John Winthrop, Governor of the Colony, described Hutchinson as "A Woman of a haughty and fierce carriage, of a nimble wit and active spirit and a very voluble tongue" (Prince Society Publications, 1894, p. 158). Hutchinson's ease and skill as a communicator were, in part, her crime, as was her usurpation of the male prerogative of speaking to an assembled audience. This violated the norms for acceptable womanly behavior. Women were not supposed to be as inherently facile at communicating as men. Consequently, when they spoke in public, they were considered impious or immodest.

In anticipation of a negative reaction, some early women speakers chose to apologize to their audience for the uncharacteristic act. Priscilla Mason said in her Salutatory Oration at the Young Ladies' Academy of Philadelphia on May 15, 1793, "A female, young and inexperienced, addressing a promiscuous assembly is a novelty which requires an apology, as some may suppose. I therefore, with submission beg issue to offer a few thoughts on the vindication of female eloquence" (Berkin and Norton, 1979, pp. 89-90). Mason went on to propose that speech, even in public settings, need not be antithetical to current notions of femininity. However, most of Mason's eighteenth and nineteenth century contemporaries vociferously disagreed.

With the coming of industrialization in the nineteenth century, historians affirm that ". . . role divisions and sexual stereotypes were permanently imprinted in the American popular mind" (Ryan, 1975, p. 75). The vast majority of licensed doctors and educators were male. Most of these men believed, and convinced the populace, that the female brain and internal organs would be injured by sustained intellectual effort. Nevertheless, women reformers, abolitionists and women's rights activists embarked upon public speaking tours.

Two of the first American women to successfully challenge the notion that public speaking was unfeminine were abolitionists Sarah and Angelina Grimke. Daughters of a South Carolina slave holding family, the Grimkes moved north to Philadelphia and joined the Quakers, the only large religious denomination in the nineteenth century to allow women to become ordained as ministers. The Grimkes were invited by the American Anti-Slavery Society to speak at what were to be small parlor gatherings of women in New York. At their first meeting, more than three hundred women showed up. On subsequent occasions, men attended as well, and the Grimkes were soon addressing mixed audiences. As with other women who were political activists, people were as much outraged by the audacity of a woman speaking to a mixed audience as offended by anything she might say. In a reaction against the Grimkes, the clergy published a Pastoral Letter from the Massachusetts Council of Congregational Ministers which asserted that, "When woman assumes the place and tone of man as a public reformer . . . she yields the power which God has given her for protection, and her character becomes unnatural" (The Liberator, 1837).

Increasingly throughout the nineteenth century, other American women risked being regarded as "unnatural" as they stood up to speak out on such social and political issues as abolition, temperance, women's right to education and women's right to vote. In fact, the movement for women's rights in the United States was, from the beginning, intimately tied to the struggle by women to speak out on their own behalf.

In 1840, when American abolitionists Lucretia Mott and Elizabeth Cady Stanton met in London at the World Anti-Slavery

Convention, they were mortified to find that women were not allowed to participate in the proceedings and were forced to sit passively behind a curtain. These women who had worked so courageously for the abolitionist cause were denied the right to speak at the convention to which they and their spouses had been invited. As a result of this outrage, they vowed to organize a convention that would protest against what Stanton called ". . . the injustice which had brooded for ages over the character and destiny of half the human race" (Martin, 1972, p. 42). The denial of speech was a paradigm for the other injustices women suffered. Eight years later, Stanton and Mott led the Seneca Falls Convention. Most historians cite this event as the origin of the organized women's movement in the United States.

Even on this momentous occasion, the prejudice against women communicators was as strong as the reaction to the speakers' message. Stanton's husband, abolitionist Henry B. Stanton, threatened to leave town if Elizabeth delivered a speech in which she proposed demanding the vote for women. Henry Stanton did leave town, and the long, scholarly, eloquent speech that Elizabeth Cady Stanton delivered was prefaced by an apology. Stanton said to her audience, "I should feel exceedingly diffident to appear before you at this time, having never before spoken in public, were I not nerved by a sense of right and duty" (cited in Flexner, 1968, pp. 76-77).

Stanton's "diffidence" was understandable given that many of her contemporaries believed that a woman speaking publicly was compromising her modesty, purity and virtue. The women of Stanton's time were expected to "noiselessly" follow their husband's lead.

Nonetheless, there were a few notable exceptions. Stanton's contemporary, activist Lucy Stone, was one of the earliest American women who deliberately planned to undertake a career as a public speaker. After graduating from Oberlin College in 1847, Stone became a professional anti-slavery lecturer. In 1855, when Stone married fellow abolitionist Henry Blackwell, the *Boston Post* published a poem that ended, "A name like Curtius' shall be his/on Fame's loud trumpet blown/ who with a wedding kiss shuts up/ the mouth of Lucy Stone" (Flexner, 1968, p. 70).

Fortunately, the Blackwell-Stone marriage appears to have been a union in which Blackwell supported and encouraged

Stone's activism and public speaking. However, implicit in the anonymous verse quoted above is the belief that husbands may "shut up" their wives, and that women who talk too much should be silenced.

Political scientist Nannerl O. Keohane (1981) has asserted that, "The power of such prescriptive silence is such that when women do speak, their speech sounds strange. It deviates from the norm of masculinity in timbre and in pattern. . . . And the words of women are consistently devalued in group settings, not heard, assumed to be trivial, not attended to" (pp. 91-92).

Unlike the women activists mentioned above, the *stereotypically* feminine speaker is soft spoken, self-effacing, and compliant. More emotional than logical, she is prone to be disorganized and subjective.

It is obvious that this image of women is biased and restrictive. Let us look in greater detail at these limitations in the feminine stereotype.

Limitations of the Feminine Stereotype

1. *She is soft spoken.*

Women, like children, have been taught that it is preferable for them to be seen rather than to be heard. When heard, female voices are apt to be considered abrasive or displeasing, and their words devoid of serious meaning.

If we examine some of the more pejorative adjectives that can be used to describe speakers, we see that in addition to Hutchinson's "voluble" tongue, a voice may be considered carping, brassy, nagging, shrill, strident or grating. Conversing may be referred to as babbling, blabbing, gabbing or chattering. Although these terms are not specifically gender identified, they are commonly used to describe the speech behavior of females and each implies the superficial or trivial nature of the speaker's message. Many women have internalized this socially imposed stereotype; in many cases, a deeply rooted reticence to speaking out precludes them from expressing themselves in any public setting.

Sociologist Lucille Duberman (1975) has explained that "To internalize means . . . to adopt the standards of one's society as part of one's self image, so that the attitudes and behaviors

approved by the society appear to have no possible alternatives''
(p. 27). By accepting and internalizing the stereotypical view
of women as communicators, women are discouraged from using
their voice to assert a point strongly. The soft-spoken woman's
voice does not carry. She threatens no one; she may lack
sufficient force and volume to speak up effectively and
convincingly. Women who are hampered by the need to sound
feminine may adopt a high-pitched ''little girl'' voice, an
artificially ''sexy,'' breathy voice, or a volume so low as to be
barely audible. In any case, the ''soft spoken'' woman is at a
marked disadvantage if she attempts to negotiate a contract,
persuade a jury, or present a report.

2. *She is self-effacing.*

To some extent, women's messages are ignored, interrupted
and not attended to because women are taught, according to
Robin Lakoff (1975), to ''talk like a lady,'' to use disclaimers
(''This may not be right, but . . .''), weak particles (''Dear me,''
''Goodness,'' etc.), tag questions (''The book was good, wasn't
it?''), and to reflect uncertainty. When women do not employ
these tactics, they may be accused of being unfeminine; but if
they do ''talk like a lady,'' they risk not being taken seriously.
Consequently, the stereotype of the female speaker as insecure,
superficial, and weak becomes self-perpetuating. Having been
historically discouraged from speaking, women internalize the
stereotype and fear violating the norm. This fear leads to the
acculturated adoption of communicative strategies that are
hyper-polite, constructed to please by minimizing one's own
skills rather than to risk antagonizing one's audience. These are
tactics which have been associated with less powerful
individuals. When women adopt them, the perception of
women's relative weakness as communicators is confirmed.

3. *She is compliant.*

The diffidence or insecurity experienced by the speaker who
is conscious of her violation of societal norms may be manifested
in several ways. Rather than be labeled ''unnatural'' or
''unfeminine,'' a woman may engage in what Janet Stone and
Jane Bachner (1977) have called ''self-trivializing messages'' that
register the speaker's insecurity, doubt and eagerness to please.

The compliant speaker allows herself to be interrupted. She moves out of the way when someone approaches her. She smiles often to assure the good will of others. She maintains eye contact and listens attentively while others speak but averts her eyes when she is the focus of attention. The compliant woman demonstrates her submissiveness through these communicative behaviors, which are characteristics of subordinates in a hierarchy. Those who are perceived as, and who perceive themselves as, less powerful tend to employ verbal and nonverbal tactics calculated to appease rather than to threaten their listeners. Women who do not engage in these behaviors have often been criticized by the public.

4. *She is emotional and subjective.*

This aspect of the feminine stereotype directly affects the female speaker's credibility. A speaker is considered credible when she or he can demonstrate competence, dynamism, consistency and co-orientation with an audience. The more subjective a speaker appears, the less likely she or he seems to support a point with evidence from other acknowledged sources. Audiences regard as less credible a message built on feelings rather than on facts. Yet mathematician Evelyn Fox Keller (1983) has called into question "the mythology that casts objectivity, reason and mind as male, and subjectivity, feeling and nature as female" (p. 15). Keller suggests that we look beyond the myth of objectivity in order to examine "the influence of our own desires, wishes and beliefs" on the claims and discoveries we make (p. 16).

Nonetheless, we have been conditioned to view objectivity as superior to subjectivity. This is part of the lens through which women and men have been taught to view the world. Simone de Beauvoir (1952) wrote that "Representation of the world, like the world itself, is the work of men. They describe it from their own point of view, which they confuse with the absolute truth" (p. 133). It is from this "truth" that our masculine and feminine stereotypes have evolved.

II. Masculine Stereotypes

Background

Rhetoric is one of the oldest academic disciplines. Originating in the Western world with the Greeks, the formal study of oral discourse as a means of persuasion and of finding "truth," was based upon masculine communication models. Walter J. Ong (1972) wrote that, "Rhetoric developed in the past as a major expression of the rational level of ceremonial combat which is found among males and typically only among males at the physical level throughout the entire animal kingdom" (p. 128). Ong claimed that not only was the masculine model of communication based on confrontation and conflict but that academic education (which for centuries was the exclusive province of males until the romantic age), was consequently based on "defending a position (thesis) or attacking the position of another person" (Ong, 1972, p. 128). All disciplines were taught by this method.

In western societies, men have been reared to confront, to compete, to challenge and to win; women have been taught to acquiesce, to accommodate and to compromise. When placed within the framework of communication, this gender-linked behavior leads males to gravitate toward delivering organized public speeches and debates, while women are encouraged to mediate and to listen. In most cultures, implicit in this division of tasks is a hierarchy of values.

Historically, men have had almost exclusive access to formal language training and to education. In the Judeo-Christian tradition, men learned and spoke Hebrew and Latin. One of the dicta of Rabbinic Judaism was, "cursed be the man who teaches his daughter Torah" (Ruether, 1981, p. 52). In religion, politics and education, men were afforded the right and given the encouragement to learn, to speak what they knew, and to use their speech to achieve their desires.

Males have been taught to be logical, objective and impersonal; women have been encouraged to be subjective, self-disclosing and personal. Overwhelmingly, the "masculine" traits have been afforded greater status. Women render themselves vulnerable by their self-disclosure; men derive power from sounding authoritative and communicating facts rather than emotions.

Many communication texts employ aggressive metaphors in their discussion of rhetoric. Speakers are instructed to "arm" themselves against the other speaker's "argument"; to "win" their point by "waging an attack" on the "weak" points in their "opponent's" logic with a strong "plan of battle." This is a specifically male formula based on ancient Greek philosophers, statesmen and orators.

This tradition demonstrates how a male stereotype has developed throughout history. *The masculine model is that of a speaker who is direct, confrontative, forceful and logical; the few, well-chosen words are focused on making a particular point.*

There are two major drawbacks to this model. First, unlike the specifically "feminine" stereotypes, the male version appears to be neutral rather than gender specific. Simone de Beauvoir has explained that masculine values and behavior have been considered the desirable "human" norm, while feminine values and behavior have been regarded as aberrant and "other" (1952, p. XVI). It is, therefore, often difficult for men to see that the male generic is, in fact, the "male-specific." Consequently, men have resisted identifying the limitations of their role and expanding upon it. The limitations in the "feminine" stereotype as we have identified it are explicit. However, we need to dig deeper to uncover the negative implications in the male role.

Limitations of the Male Stereotype

1. *He is an ineffective listener.*

One deficiency in the male stereotype has been the negative association for listening. As we have established, speaking is active. Listening has often been portrayed inaccurately as passive, weak, or "feminine" behavior, since it necessitates receptivity to others. Because much of their survival has depended upon the ability to read and decode accurately the verbal and nonverbal clues of superiors, women (and other subordinates in hierarchies) have to develop their listening skills more effectively. Gloria Steinem (1983) has claimed that women's so-called "intuition" is a manifestation of their better developed listening skills.

When a man has been reared to regard his own message as paramount, he often interrupts other speakers and/or prepares his own response mentally while others are speaking rather than attending to the messages of others. In mixed-sex pairs, according to researchers Don H. Zimmerman and Candace West (1975), men overwhelmingly interrupt women.

2. *He may not express his emotions.*

Another communication weakness that Warren Farrell (1972) ironically lists among the "Ten Commandments of Masculinity" is the dictum that because men "shalt not be vulnerable," they may not express fear, weakness, sympathy, empathy or involvement" (cited in Duberman, 1975, p. 224). Because they are taught to value the logical, practical and intellectual to the exclusion of the emotional, males find it difficult to communicate emotions (except anger). When one partner is routinely more self-disclosing and, therefore, more vulnerable, the result is a hierarchical rather than an egalitarian relationship. Thus, in situations where men most desire intimacy and trust, the masculine dictum against expressing emotions may prove an enormous impediment.

3. *He makes categorical assertions.*

The masculine stereotype encourages men to be authoritative and to make sweeping claims. This behavior appears to reflect self-assurance. However, by avoiding the feminine communicative mode of qualification and indirection, men may in fact be limited by their assertions. Carol Gilligan (1982) asserts that the tendency of women to be more indirect and open to options can be an asset; this type of open communication is more than just a form of deference born of women's social subordination. As Gilligan states, "Sensitivity to the needs of others and the assumption of the responsibility for taking care lead women to attend to voices other than their own and to include in their judgement other points of view" (p. 16). When individuals sincerely desire open and honest communication among equals, they need to resist categorical assertions that reflect a preconceived mind set.

4. *He dominates the discussion.*

A final aspect of the masculine stereotype is the assumption that men speak significantly less than women. In the gender-linked communication traits mentioned earlier, research has confirmed the fact that female and male behaviors do not generally reflect the respective stereotypes. However, numerous studies have shown that the assumption that men are less talkative than women is based on fiction rather than on fact (Argyle, et al., 1968; Strodtbeck and Mann, 1956). In mixed-sex groups, men routinely speak more than women and, in fact, usually dominate the conversations. Men are more likely to introduce the topics which are discussed, to interrupt others, and to initiate the changing of topics. Much of women's talk is devoted to drawing men into conversation and offering a number of topics from which males may choose.

Furthermore, when male silence occurs in mixed-sex discussions, it does not necessarily denote listening. The withholding of speech can also imply power. Superiors need not answer subordinates, but subordinates are usually compelled to respond to superiors. However, equal "veto" power in a conversation is necessary for individuals to feel that they have established an effective communication climate. Therefore, any individual who dominates a discussion negatively influences the communication climate.

III. Nonverbal Aspects of the Stereotypes

The feminine and masculine stereotypes that we have identified thus far have nonverbal components as well. As with verbal gender-linked traits, the nonverbal distinctions also imply a power differential. Psychologist Nancy Henley (1977, p. 187) has identified gestures that communicate dominance and submission in this culture.

Dominance	Submission
Stare	Lower eyes, avert gaze, blink
Touch	Cuddle to the touch
Interrupt	Stop talking
Crowd another's space	Yield, move away
Frown, look stern	Smile
Point	Move in pointed direction; obey

We can observe that gestures of dominance are stereotypically male, and those of submission are stereotypically female. When power differences are communicated nonverbally, they are extremely difficult to isolate and to identify in context. As a result, much of how we picture gender differences appears innate rather than as a function of a pervasive, learned nonverbal communication behavior pattern.

In Chapter III, we examine specific ways that masculinity and femininity are communicated nonverbally. At this point, it is important to note that cultural stereotypes for men and women, whether communicated through verbal or nonverbal channels, are as much symbols of power or powerlessness as they are models of gender differences.

In this Chapter we have identified three important stereotypes: that of the "naturally" insecure, superficial and weak woman, and the "unnaturally" talkative, loud and abrasive one. Both of these images are limiting. We have explored the negative implications of the masculine model of a "confrontative," "logical" man of few words. For the most part, these stereotypes represent actual traits that women and men have been reared to display. To that extent, they may be considered social "fact." But since gender-linked traits are learned rather than innate behaviors, the stereotypes are also a "fiction."

The models of femininity and masculinity that we have internalized have been with us for centuries. Throughout history, women and men have been penalized for violating societal norms. Women have been called "unnatural" and "masculine;" men, "effeminate." Now, at the close of the twentieth century, it has become apparent that a rigid adherence to the sex role stereotypes is a disadvantage. We believe that individuals are capable of creating other, less limiting, more androgynous communication models. In order to accomplish this, we first must examine in greater detail the specific verbal and nonverbal behaviors through which our respective stereotypes are manifested.

Suggested Activities

A. Focus on Listening: Vocal Stereotyping

Listen to a television soap opera with which you are unfamiliar. Turn off the picture and only listen to the voices. See if you can identify the "good," "bad," "sexy," "intelligent," and "dumb" character types by their vocal qualities.

- a) What are vocal characteristics of the "good" young wife? The debutante? The manipulator? What about the tough guy? The sincere, young lover?
- b) How is socio-economic class indicated vocally?
- c) Do the characters' voices remind you of anyone you know? If so, do you have similar associations for both the character and your acquaintance because of how she or he sounds?

B. Focus on Interpersonal/Dyadic Communication and Vocal Stereotyping.

1. Keep track of individuals to whom you speak who have noticeably different speech patterns from your own. Try to use their intonation pattern and mode of articulation when you converse. Note what happens.
   - a) Is your partner aware of your adjustment?
   - b) Does she or he think you sound "natural?"
   - c) Is your partner more open and self-disclosing when you sound alike?
2. Tape a conversation between yourself and a speaker with a different native language. Listen to the pitch and intonation patterns, and note the differences.
   - a) What attitudes or character traits would these vocal behaviors connote for native-born American English speakers?
   - b) Have you assumed that your partner is shy, argumentative, elusive, or confrontative on the basis of an ethnocentric evaluation of vocal traits?

chapter **2**

Vocal and Verbal Behavior

> [Woman] must have the skill to incline us to do everything
> which her sex will not enable her to do for herself . . . she
> should also have the art, by her own conversation, actions,
> looks and gestures, to communicate those sentiments which
> are agreeable to (men), without seeming to intend it.
>
> —Jean Jacques Rousseau
> *Emilius*

As the quote above illustrates, women and men have been taught to use language and nonverbal communication differently and for different purposes. (Did you just react with surprise when you read "women and men" instead of the more customary "men and women?" If so, you are starting to realize how ingrained habitual linguistic patterns become.)

When we published the first edition of this book (1985) the research supporting the existence of gender differences in communication was just coming to the attention of various disciplines. We recognized then, as we do today, that many of the differences observed in men's and women's communicative behavior were essentially differences in relative power between the sexes in a given situational context. In other words, Speaker A may act or speak in one way when communicating with his/her significant other and in another manner when interacting with her/his employee, supervisor, or student.

Thus, as we examine some of the variables that comprise a communicative exchange, remember that individuals employ various *interactional strategies* depending upon the situation and the person with whom one communicates. Every strategy is employed for a particular purpose or goal; the speaker may or may not be conscious of that objective. Just as it is significant to examine differences and similarities in the verbal, vocal and nonverbal strategies women and men adopt, so is it important to keep in mind that the *goal or intent of an interaction* may be different for women and for men. As Kramerae (1981) noted, when women and men speak to each other, their intentions may be different. One's goal may be to build rapport while the other attempts to assert or resist control; one may communicate so as to maintain relationships or for the purpose of imposing one's will. Given the relative positions of women and men in a particular society, the strategies communicators adopt to achieve their various goals may vary by sex.

No variable in isolation will give us a complete picture of the similarities and differences in the ways men and women communicate. In this chapter we will investigate research on the ways women and men sound (paralinguistic or vocal messages), the linguistic choices (verbal messages) we make, and the interpretations or meanings that have been offered for these differences.

I. Vocal Behaviors

A. Articulation; or "How correct do you sound?"

Articulation comes from the Latin word for joint. It refers to the joining together of the organs of articulation (e.g., lips, tongue, teeth, glottis, etc.) so as to chop the breath stream into individual sounds. All speakers do not produce and pronounce speech sounds in the same way. For example, if one neglects to place his or her tongue tip between the upper and lower teeth in an attempt to produce a "th" sound (θ or ð), the result may sound like "t" or "d" as in the case of the speaker who says "dese tree tings" for "these three things."

Women are largely judged by their appearance, and speech

strongly affects how they appear to others. Numerous studies have established that women are more likely to use standard phonetic grammatical forms than men. Males of similar socio-economic groups employ more casual and colloquial speech than females. Roger Shuy's (1967) study of seven hundred Detroit residents demonstrated that males were more likely to nasalize the (æ) vowel and drop "ing" endings in favor of the more casual "in'." For example: "The man was walkin' and talkin.'" William Labov's (1973) studies in New York and Chicago, Peter Trudgill's (1975) research on British speakers in Norwich, England, and Walter Wolfram's (1969) studies of Black speakers in Detroit all indicate that women in each respective group use more standard forms.

Further research by Levine and Crockett (1979) on North Carolina speakers and Milroy (1980) on speakers from working class communities in Belfast, Ireland have continued to evidence sex differences, with the women's articulation more closely approximating that of the standard or prestige dialect. In addition, both Levine and Crockett and Milroy noted that men and women's pronunciation was most different from each other in working class communities with their own dense social networks which may exert localized linguistic pressures on men to sound as if they "belong." Perhaps even more surprising is Beverly Hartford's (1976) finding of phonological differences in the English of adolescent Chicanas and Chicanos. Hartford found that even in a second language, the females were more likely than the males to adopt the prestige forms of speech which are associated with middle class native speakers and upward mobility.

Trudgill (1975) offers two explanations for this phenomenon. He believes that because women within each social strata are subordinate to men, they must "secure and signal their status linguistically" (1975, p. 91). Second, (p. 91) since less formal, more working-class pronunciation is associated with toughness and masculinity, women are encouraged to talk like "ladies."

Having taught and lived in working-class environments, it has been our experience that many males have been raised to believe that studying and improving one's articulation is an effeminate undertaking. They seem to fear that attention to standard or prestige grammar and articulation will cause others to consider them less masculine. Yet the ability to employ standard articulatory and grammatical forms is of considerable importance for males as well as for females. Because prestige forms are equated with higher socioeconomic status, males who resist adopting standard speech in professional or public settings may find their career options impeded. When applying for a job, fighting a traffic ticket, looking for an apartment, or dealing with other forms of authority, the ability to assume standard speech can be considered an asset.

B. Pitch; or "How big do you sound?"

A fundamental difference in the way that women and men sound is that women's voices are generally higher pitched than men's. It is partially the size of one's vocal tract that determines pitch. Over the past several years, numerous female students who have registered for our Women as Speakers and Gender and Intercultural Communication classes, bemoaned the fact that nature had saddled them with squeaky, high-pitched, "little girl" voices. However, studies by Ignatius Mattingly (1966) and Jacqueline Sachs, Philip Lieberman and Donna Erickson (1973) indicate that the differences in male and female pitch are much greater than anatomical variations logically could explain. Mattingly studied three classes of speakers: men, women and children. He found that male and female speakers of the same dialect tend to form vowels differently thereby affecting the pitch. Mattingly concluded this was a social and linguistic convention. Sachs, *et al.* studied preadolescent children with larynxes of the same size relative to their weight. Adult judges were able to identify the sex of the children solely by listening to tapes of their voices. The researchers hypothesized that, regardless of the size of the larynx and vocal cords, males and females may be adjusting their pitch to fit cultural expectations and stereotypes. This adjustment can be seen as well in bilingual speakers whose pitch alters with the language they are speaking.

A large person would be expected to have longer, thicker vocal cords and therefore would speak with a lower pitch. A small person with shorter, thinner vocal cords would be expected to have a higher pitched voice. However, individuals may change their pitch by changing the position of their lips when producing vowel sounds. More open lips shorten the vocal tract and thus raise the pitch. For example, women who speak while smiling produce higher pitched sounds than those who do not. Although Sachs et al. do not discount the fact that hormonal differences may account for some variation, they speculate that by adjusting the way sounds are produced, *males tend to make themselves sound as though they are larger and females as though they are smaller than the articulatory mechanism alone would suggest.* (Later in this book we will discuss the extent to which size communicates power nonverbally.) Thus, by adopting excessively high-pitched voices, women are limiting themselves. Women who have assumed this vocal type sound giddy and childish, and they are frequently not taken seriously. The high-pitched childish voice not only diminishes them in size, it diminishes their credibility.

Erving Goffman (1977) has examined the ways men and women are taught to display gender. He found that frequently the verbal and nonverbal interactions between women and men have *produced* differences. Goffman describes numerous interactions—from bear hugs to threats via pushes or other forms of "teasing"—whereby males encourage females "to provide a full-voiced rendition of the plight to which her sex is presumably prone." Thus, a female's assumption of a higher than natural pitch may be a behavior learned and reinforced in a multitude of interactions throughout her life.

For many years women were denied access to careers in broadcasting on the pretext that the higher-pitched female voice did not sound serious enough, although in France the female voice has been *preferred* for news broadcasting. Here in the United States, we have grown considerably from the time when the only female voices on the nightly news were those of the "cute" (i.e., not serious) "weather girls." Interestingly enough, when broadcast weather predictions became more scientific, the weather girl was replaced by a male meteorologist. However, we still tend to regard the lower-pitched male voice as the voice of authority. Overwhelmingly, male voices are used in commercial voiceovers, even for household products that are purchased and used almost exclusively by women.

Lower-pitched voices seem to be regarded more positively by

both women and men. Women's voices used in the broadcast media tend to be lower-pitched than those of the female population at large. In fact, William Austin (1965) found that the act of *imitating a person of either sex* with a derogatory, high-pitched feminine voice was perceived as an infuriating "act of aggression." Since an artificially high pitch connotes timidity, childishness and/or weakness, it is not surprising that most individuals would be insulted to be depicted in this fashion.

What then are the implications for women whose natural voices are somewhat higher than those of men? First, women need to be aware of whether they are diminishing themselves by employing a higher pitch than necessary. If so, they must examine the settings in which they are most likely to use their "little girl" voice. Does this occur most frequently with friends, lovers, parents, or employers? Is it a subconscious strategy women adopt when they fear that their message might threaten the person with whom they speak? It may be that women adopt this guise of powerlessness when they anticipate resentment of their strength. Second, speakers can practice exercises to lower their pitch. (See suggested activities at the end of the chapter). And third, all of us need to guard against judging individuals as if their pitch were a barometer of their capabilities, intelligence or maturity.

C. Intonation; or "How certain to you sound?"

Related to pitch is the more specific area of intonation or inflection. While pitch refers to the general high or low quality of the voice, intonation refers to the pitch swings or changes within a phrase or sentence. Every language has its own intonation patterns. American English speakers usually employ a rising intonation for most questions (except those preceded by interrogative words, e.g., *who, what, when, where, why,* and *how*), to express hesitancy or uncertainty, and to indicate incompleteness of a thought (as in listing items in a series). A falling intonation is used to give commands, state facts, and to ask questions.

Sally McConnell-Ginet (1978) has hypothesized that the basic intonational system may be used differently by women than by men. Women are more likely to use certain intonational patterns that feature upward inflections and a wider range of speaking pitches that change more frequently than do men. American male English speakers tend to avoid those patterns which have been stigmatized as feminine, except in an intentional deviation from stereotyped behavior in order to present oneself as "gay" or in a hostile imitation of women (Austin 1965, Terango 1966). In fact, Terango found that a greater variety of pitches employed by a speaker, coupled with the rapidity of the change from one pitch to another, was a more salient marker of "feminine" speech than the overall highness of the speaker's pitch.

Similarly, Ruth Brend (1975) found that most men employ only three levels of intonation contrasts, while a majority of women use four. Men tend to avoid final patterns that do not end at their lowest pitch level. For example, the female professional is much more likely to invite someone into her office with an upward inflected "Come in." Her male colleague's "Come in" with a downward glide may sound more like a command than a polite request.

Robin Lakoff (1975) characterized women's traditional intonation patterns as reflective of hesitancy, uncertainty, or lack of assertiveness. Lakoff found that when offering a declarative answer to a question, women often use a rising pattern, which sounds as though they were asking for confirmation, approval, or doubting their own answer. For example, in response to the question, "When are you free to meet with me?" the female speaker may reply "In about . . . twenty minutes . . . ?" Had she replied "In twenty minutes." with a downward pattern, her message would imply that the addressee had no choice but to wait. This intonation pattern would support a superior, rather than a subordinate position. However, the stereotypically feminine rising pitch pattern sounds more polite in that it appears as if the speaker is leaving the decision open rather than imposing her decision upon the addressee.

However, subsequent researchers have called into question such bipolar interpretations of intonation patterns. Carole Edelsky (1979) found that women responding to a question about which they were certain were more likely to employ a rising-falling-rising intonation when speaking with a female interviewer than with a male interviewer. Edelsky interpreted her subjects' rising intonation as a desire for a longer exchange rather than as a marker of insecurity. Similarly, Barrie Thorne (1975) noted the extensive use of the high rising intonation among feminists speaking with one another. Thorne attributed this style to "an invitation to others to speak, emphasizing the collectivity of the group and underscoring a speaker's desire not to present herself as a "heavy" (quoted in McConnell-Ginet, n. 17).

A third interpretation of the high rising upward swing such as in the female speaker's utterance of "In...twenty minutes...? is that the rising intonation may be reflective of a further question which is implied vocally rather than explicitly stated by the speaker. Questions such as "Is twenty minutes alright for your schedule?" of "Do you think twenty minutes will leave us enough time to complete our business?" or incompletely articulated thoughts, such as "I am busy at this moment. I estimate the work will take twenty minutes to complete, but it may take longer" may be communicated paralinguistically by the upward swing in intonation (McConnell-Ginet 1975; Ladd 1980).

Earlier researchers were quick to label the upward swing and frequent and rapid pitch changes which characterize female speech as definitive markers of insecurity, incompleteness, hesitancy or doubt. The more monotone delivery of male speech was viewed as a norm from which more expressive women's voices departed. Just as we need to resist adopting the stereotypes that define several pitch patterns as indicative of "hysteria" or "whining," we should resist characterizing males' lack of vocal variety as a sign of "keeping one's cool" or emotional detachment.

We must become cognizant of the extent to which vocal behavior is interpreted as a signal of the speaker's attitude about him or herself and toward the listener. We need also be aware that in different languages and dialects, pitch, intonation patterns and degree of precision in articulation carry different connotations. The English as a second language instructor who encourages opposite sex foreign students merely to imitate her or his pitch and intonation patterns without understanding the social connotations of these patterns may be compounding rather than alleviating problems. In our attitudes about men, women, and native speakers of other languages, we need to be careful not to confuse how we sound with what we mean to say.

II. Verbal Constructs

For several decades, researchers have been attempting to determine to what extent the words speakers use and the way they arrange their utterances syntactically is influenced by gender. Sociolinguists have much evidence that geographic region, socioeconomic factors, educational level and ethnic identification can all impact the dialect we speak. Researchers such as Lakoff (1975), Kramer (1974) and Thorne and Henley (1975) first proposed the possibility that women may speak a "women's language" or "genderlect" that is characterized by the usage of certain vocabulary, qualifiers, disclaimers, tag questions and compound requests.

In the first edition of this book we reported those findings uncritically. However, subsequent research has pointed to new and more complex explanations for the gender differentials in some of the findings reported earlier. First, it appears that there is less homogeneity among women and men than was previously assumed. Second, the person with whom one is communicating and the situational context influence verbal strategies as well. Speech, in both its vocal and verbal dimensions, is a marker of in-group solidarity. Part of the metacommunicative message that runs through many verbal exchanges is an attempt at an unconscious matching, as if one were saying "See, we speak the same "language," we can understand each other. So a male or female speaker in a personal or professional situation with equal status may elect one set of verbal constructs and employ an entirely different strategy when communicating with a person over whom she or he has authority or to whom she or he shows deference. As you read about the following constructs, examine your own behavior. Do you employ different strategies with same or opposite sex friends? With elder family members? In the classroom? In the workplace?

A. Qualifiers; or "I sort of think maybe you know what I mean." and Intensifiers; or "I'm sooo very, very glad to hear it."

The use of qualifiers (such as sort of, kind of, rather, really, I think, I guess) has been found by researchers to be more common in the speech of women than in men. Crosby and Nyquist (1977) found that although role relationships influenced the use of qualifiers, women more than men qualified their messages. A qualifier softens the statement in which it appears. "I am sort of disappointed in your work this quarter" sounds less devastating to a listener than an unqualified statement. Even the words "actually" and "really," or "very" and "so" which may appear at first glance to intensify an expression, do, in fact, soften it. "I *really* don't want to be disturbed" is less assertive than "I don't want to be disturbed." The need for "actually" and "really" may imply that the speaker believes that she or he will not be taken seriously without the added emphasis.

Some researchers, like William O'Barr (1982), have analyzed the use of qualifiers, intensifiers, tag questions, and disclaimers (see below) in the courtroom and contend that these constructs are indicative of powerlessness and are more related to socioeconomic class and educational experience than to gender. However, Patricia Bradley (1981) found that the use of qualifiers was only perceived negatively when women used these linguistic devices. When men used qualifiers, they were seen as being warm and polite rather than weak and unassertive.

When we qualify statements, they sound less categorical and less likely to offend listeners. Newcombe and Arnkoss (1979) found that qualifiers may be appropriate when we want to convey warmth, politeness or consideration. However, if they are employed routinely—whenever one needs to take a verbal stand—these "crutches" may get in the way. If listeners perceive a speaker to be "too soft" or not authoritative enough, using qualifiers will further diminish the speaker's credibility.

B. Disclaimers; or "This probably doesn't mean anything, but . . ."

Disclaimers are excuses or apologies offered by a speaker before she or he makes a remark. According to Eakins and Eakins (1978) women are more likely than men to use disclaimers such as "This probably isn't important, but . . ." or "I'm not really sure about this, however . . ."

By using these expressions, the speaker attempts to distance her- or himself from the claim rather than to stand behind it. The disclaimer serves in part as an apology for speaking. It also serves as a plea to an audience not to associate the speaker too closely with the message. This protective device reassures the speaker that her or his message may be rejected without the speaker being rejected.

When individuals use disclaimers, their message is weakened before it is uttered. The disclaimer leads the audience to believe either the speaker lacks knowledge, is unprepared or lacks strong conviction. Disclaimers are found more frequently in women's speech than in men's. They also are found often in the speech of non-native English speakers. Disclaimers manifest the speaker's perception that one has to apologize in advance to gain the goodwill of an audience that would otherwise not be receptive.

In our work with female students and with non-native English speakers, we have encouraged them to eliminate disclaimers from their speech. The use of a disclaimer may be a strategy to ingratiate oneself to a possibly prejudiced or inattentive audience. However, in addition to speakers being advised to avoid such strategies, listeners also need to be aware that their responses to speakers may be encouraging the use of disclaimers. Listeners bear a responsibility to demonstrate verbally and nonverbally that they are receptive to the speaker.

When women and nonnative English speakers are made to feel that they are being listened to willingly and with concentration, they will be less likely to punctuate their remarks with disclaimers. While we encourage women to abandon the self-effacing strategy, we recommend that listeners ask themselves, "What have I done or am I doing to make this speaker feel that she or he is not worthy of my attention?"

C. Tag Questions; or "This is what I meant, isn't it?"

Robin Lakoff (1975) has defined a tag question as "midway between an outright statement and a yes/no question." An example of a tag question is "We have an appointment at three o'clock, don't we?" The tag "don't we?" is an attempt to gain confirmation from one's listener. The speaker is avoiding committing him/herself to an outright statement while trying to hedge against one of the possible responses to a bipolar (yes/no) question. If the speaker asks "Do we have an appointment at three o'clock?" she risks equally the possibilities of receiving a negative or affirmative response. The tag question is also, therefore, a form of leading question in that the respondent is led in a particular direction.

Lakoff claimed that women use this construction more frequently than do men and that its use is a marker of uncertainty. Tag questions have also been seen as a request for approval of either the speaker or the speaker's message. Subsequent findings have been complex and contradictory. Some researchers, such as Fishman (1980) and McMillan et al. (1977), conducted studies where women were found to use more tag questions than did men.

Others, such as Dubois and Crouch (1977) and Johnson (1980) found men in professional contexts using more tag questions than did their female colleagues. However, these researchers offer a variety of divergent interpretations for the tag question construct. Pamela Fishman, whose 1980 study found women employing more tag questions than did their male partners, saw the use of tags as an attempt on the woman's part to gain some response from the male partner. Women, doing more of the interaction work in maintaining the heterosexual relationships she studied, used tags to engage their partners in dialogue, not to convey uncertainty. Johnson (1980) also found that the use of tags, by requesting responses from listeners, help sustain interaction. The tag, like the French "n'est-ce pas?" or the Spanish "¿Es verdad?" may be an attempt to keep the conversational ball rolling and thereby to maintain relationships.

Lakoff also noted the use of tag questions in small talk. There are few icebreakers in the entry-acquaintance phase of a relationship that are more innocuous than "It's a nice day, isn't it?" The use of tag questions may be a polite attempt to engage in nonthreatening conversation.

Arliss (1991), Borisoff and Merrill (1985), and Dubois and Crouch (1977) all observe that tag questions may be used in an intimidating or overbearing way to assure a response which negates the listener's possibility of opposition. Depending upon the intonation, it may be condescending to ask "You won't do that again, will you?" or "I told you to finish this report by Thursday, didn't I?"

Speakers need to become aware of their reasons for electing to use tag questions and the various connotations, from uncertainty and insecurity to condescension that such usage may imply to listeners. Although the tag form is indirect, it is neither inherently weak nor strong.

D. Compound Requests; or "How many words shall I use to make my wishes known?"

Despite stereotypes to the contrary, women often have more difficulty voicing requests and demands than men. Individuals who are accustomed to wielding considerable personal power are more likely to use imperatives than are subordinates. For example, "Type this now!" is a command issued by a speaker who assumes that his or her authority is such that the addressee is compelled to comply. On the other hand, "Please type this now" and "Will you type this now?" are both requests. The addressee is being asked to go along with the speaker but is free to refuse.

Lakoff maintains that women tend to compound their requests by asking either "Will/Can you please type this now?" or "Won't you please type this now?" The more a request is compounded, the more polite it sounds, because the listener has increasingly greater latitude to refuse the request. The most indirect request, "If it's not too much trouble, won't you please type this now?" is worded negatively to imply the greater possibility of the addressee's refusal.

Speakers and listeners of both sexes should be aware of how they choose to phrase their requests. Those who routinely employ indirect compound forms may find that, on occasion, a more direct, less apologetic tone is more expedient. However, speakers who characteristically use imperatives need to take responsibility for how they phrase their messages as well as for what they say. Many male speakers, in particular, are baffled when their listeners bridle against being *ordered* to do something that the speaker *intended* as a *request* rather than as a command.

Both strategies—direct and polite—are necessary skills to master.

E. Vocabulary Differences, or "Which words are whose?"

Certain words and categories of words appear more frequently in the speech of women in a given social, economic and geographical context than in the speech of men. Adverbs of intensity (such as *awfully, terribly, pretty, quite, so*) and the adjectives *charming, lovely, adorable, dreadful, ghastly* and *divine* appear more common in the speech of female American English speakers than of American men. We do not observe this same distinction in the lexicon of male and female British English speakers, however.

Steckler and Cooper (1980) also found that women used more specific color terms than did men. Words for colors like *taupe, mauve, beige, lavender* and *violet* are not common in men's speech. Men are more likely to use combination terms, such as "reddish brown" rather than "rust." Males are not expected to discuss the "lovely mauve drapes" in the conference room or the "streaks of lavender" in the sunset. When men do use words that are stereotypically part of the female lexicon, they risk being considered effeminate.

Some theorists believe that the words women use lead listeners to regard them as trivial and superficial because of the attention paid to subtle distinctions and details—such as color gradations. However, we could argue that the ability to discern and to describe more subtle differences in color is a strength in women's speech, not a detriment. Nonetheless, it is important for female speakers to note that their message is likely to be regarded as superficial and irrelevant when they use such phrases as "the taupe attache case," for example. The problem does not lie in the words but in the *connotation* these words have for the listeners who hear them.

Men are afforded the right to use specific words that, until recently, were rarely present in women's speech. Forceful expletives like *damn* and *hell* are considered much more acceptable in men's speech than in women's. Women risk being considered unfeminine when they use these words. Instead, women have been encouraged to be polite and to use such expressions as "dear me," "oh my," and "goodness." These particles are less forceful than those allowed men, and their use tends to weaken or to render trivial the expression which follows. For example, it would sound ludicrous for the female executive to say, "Dear me, you mean we lost the multimillion dollar contract?" or for the female attorney to remark, "Oh, goodness. I hope we don't have another hung jury."

Increasingly, women in all fields are more likely to employ the expletives found in male speech to convey strong emotions. Men rarely, however, use "women's" particles. Men are likely to be stigmatized for their use of feminine words. As Lakoff explains, "The language of the favored group, the group that holds power . . . is generally adopted by the other group, and not vice versa"(1975, p. 10).

Men and women have been taught to use language differently. For women, communication is a social medium. Women have been raised to use communication as a mechanism for creating bonds. Men have been encouraged to communicate primarily to exchange information. Tag questions, qualifiers, disclaimers, and intonation patterns that sound as though the speaker is requesting rather than commanding are strategies common to women's speech. These verbal and vocal behaviors are considered less direct but more polite than the corresponding patterns males tend to employ. These are not, unfortunately, as two equal options. It must be remembered that the *need to be polite* is in itself a signal of a *power* imbalance. Subordinates who fear alienating their superiors are required to be polite. Politeness is often a strategy for gaining or maintaining favor. Those already powerful are not compelled to be polite. They can, therefore, afford to be direct.

Brown and Levinson's (1978) discussion of politeness strategies presents a useful typology. Brown and Levinson assert that members of dominated and muted groups (including women) tend to engage in politeness strategies that affirm commonality when speaking with each other. However, politeness strategies based on avoidance and deference are more commonly used when communicating with dominant groups.

In this text, we do not propose one absolute model of politeness or of directedness for speakers of both sexes, nor do

we wish to reinforce sex role stratified differences in speech. We
see neither model as inherently weak nor strong. Rather, we hope
that all individuals might increase their repertoire of strategies
and responses.

III. Verbal and Vocal Behaviors in Interaction

Thus far, we have been discussing individual vocal and verbal
behaviors, but speaking is a dynamic exchange between two or
more people. We will now explore the behaviors that occur in
interactions between speakers.

Dyadic communication refers to communication between two
individuals. Men and women are engaged in mixed sex dyads
as friends, lovers, spouses, colleagues, employers and
employees, clinicians and patients, teachers and students, etc.
(In Chapter IV we discuss the specific applications of dyadic
communication in the professional setting.)

One person speaks; another listens, comments on what she
or he has heard, and offers a message which is, in turn, heard
and responded to by the first speaker. A simple conversation?
Perhaps. However, when the members of the dyad are opposite
sexes, often a hierarchy of power is established and maintained.
In mixed sex dyads who talks more? By what tactics (such as
interruption or refusal to discuss a topic offered) does one
speaker seize control of a conversation, gain the "floor,"
negotiate for speaker turn-taking, and affirm or disconfirm the
contributions of her/his conversational partner?

A. Talk Time

Contrary to stereotypes, much research on male and female
interactions in settings and relationships as diverse as the labora-
tory, the home, married couples (Kenkel, 1963), colleagues,
students (Duncan and Fiske 1977), complete strangers (Marlatt
1970), university faculty meetings (Eakins and Eakins 1978),
professional conferences (Swacker 1976) and jury deliberations
indicates that men talk for a longer amount of time than the
women with whom they interact. Some researchers, like Fred
Strodtbeck (in his studies on jury deliberation, found power and

status variables as well; men and persons of higher status spoke more than women and persons of lower status. Even when expertise is taken into consideration, Leet-Pellegrini (1980) found that male experts talked more than female experts. How do we account for the popular stereotype that women talk more than do men?

B. Topic Initiation and Topic Selection

Numerous studies have established that in mixed sex dyads women work harder than do men at asking questions and attempting to initiate topics (Fishman 1977, 1982). In many dyads, or in mixed-sex small groups, women have a hard time getting the floor or getting topics of their choosing discussed. Women and persons with less power may offer and attempt to initiate numerous different topics, but the male or person in a more dominant position, frequently selects the topics actually discussed by ignoring some conversational overtures and responding to others. Some researchers define *topic initiation* to include the mere mentioning of a new topic; others refer to the successful selection of that topic by all conversational partners. Thus, the data in this area may at first appear contradictory (Aries 1976, 1982). As Fishman (1982, p. 91) notes:

> In a sense, every remark or turn at speaking should be seen as an attempt to interact. It may be an attempt to open or close a conversation. It may be a bid to continue interaction, to respond to what went before, and elicit a further remark from one's partner. Some attempts succeed; others fail. For an attempt to succeed, the other party must be willing to do further interactional work. That other person has the power to turn an attempt into a conversation or to stop it dead.

Fishman notes than women, like the children studied by Sacks (1972), use questions to gain attention and insure a response from their conversational partners. Sacks noted children's tendencies to initiate conversations with the question "D'ya know what?" Fishman found that women were also more likely than men to preface their remarks with the statement "This is interesting . . ."

These expressions may reflect a speaker's perceived need to

gain the attention of a listener by provoking interest or attesting to the worthiness of the remark to follow — attention the speaker might not otherwise secure. In numerous studies, women offered more conversational openings than did men; however, fewer of the topics women attempted to initiate were actually selected.

An interesting study by Courtwright, Millar and Rogers-Millar (1979) relates the degree of domineeringness of marital partners with the tendency on the part of the less dominant spouse to ask more questions rather than to offer assertions and opinions. Courtwright *et al.*, found that the more dominant the husband when compared with the wife, the more questions asked by the wife. However, in the case of more dominant wives, husbands did not necessarily ask more questions.

C. Interruptions and Overlaps

One of the most disputed interaction patterns is the interruption. Interrupting another individual before he or she has finished speaking is a clear sign, according to Nichols (1948), of ineffective listening. Speakers who are interrupted frequently feel dominated, disregarded or muted by the interjection of another speaker before they have finished their "conversational turn."

West and Zimmerman (1975, 1977, 1982), Eakins and Eakins (1978) and Leet Pellegrini (1980) all found evidence that in mixed sex conversations between couples, colleagues and adult strangers, men overwhelmingly interrupt women. However Kennedy and Camden's (1983) and Dindia's (1987) studies of college students did not find males more frequently interrupting females. In studies of families, Greif (1980) and Berko, Gleason and Greif (1983) found that fathers were more likely to interrupt children than were mothers, and both parents were more likely to interrupt girls than boys. Some researchers found women were more frequently interrupted than were men, regardless of whether women or men were doing the interrupting (Kennedy 1980; Spender, 1980; Willis and Williams 1976).

Many theorists and researchers have equated interruptions with attempts at conversational dominance. However, not all incidents of simultaneous speech are attempts to interrupt and control a conversation. As Kennedy (1980) and Beattie (1981) among others note, speakers may be overlapping when they express agreement and support for the previous speaker's remark or when they jump into a conversation a few syllables ahead of their conversational turn. Dindia (1987) attributes interruptions to conversational errors or awkwardness that may occur with greater frequency in mixed sex conversations.

West and Zimmerman (1982) attempt to distinguish between those overlaps in conversation which facilitate a conversation and those which disrupt the previous speaker's turn. This distinction is significant. Few speakers feel anything other than encouragement at a conversational partner's interjection of "Yeah" or "Really?" while they are speaking. These interjections encourage a speaker to continue, rather than to give up the floor. When analyzing the interrupting behavior of any conversational partner, it is important to consider the relationship between listening and interrupting. Also, as the above studies indicate, the context and status of conversational interactants is a salient feature in interruptions. Persons with less power are more frequently interrupted.

D. Vocalizers and Minimal Responses

Vocalizers and minimal responses such as "mm-hmmm, uh huh, I see, yeah" are important parts of conversational interaction since they are frequently employed to signal attention and interest. Nichols asserted that demonstrating interest is a sign of effective listening. How we demonstrate interest, however, is also a matter of socialization.

Anthropologists Dale Mintz and Ruth Borker (1982) explained that men and women learn to use vocalizers differently. Women use vocalizers along with nonverbal indicators of interest such as head-nodding far more frequently than do men (Hirschman 1973, 1974). Women are more likely to use these strategies to indicate that they are listening and to encourage the speaker to continue. Some researchers assert that because men equate these behaviors with signals of agreement, they use them less frequently. They reserve the use of vocalizers for those instances when they agree with a speaker. Other theorists like Fishman

(1982) and Arliss (1991) claim that the use of minimal responses may display disinterest, particularly when they are timed after a partner's lengthy remarks and delivered in a slightly delayed manner. Fishman finds the disconfirming use of minimal responses more common in the speech of men than women.

Whatever the actual listening and attending behavior of men and women, women's dissatisfaction with the listening of their male partners is a well-documented fact. One of the questions in Shere Hite's (1987) study of over four thousand American women and their love relationships was "What does your partner do that makes you the maddest?" Seventy-seven percent responded, "He doesn't listen." Further, 59 percent reported that men interrupt them, 84 percent said that men often seemed not to hear, 69 percent said that men generally did not listen or ask about activities and 83 percent remarked that men only seemed to listen at the beginning of relationships. Interestingly, 85 percent of Hite's respondents said that the most wonderful quality of their friendships with other women was the ability to talk openly and freely without being judged. Eighty-two percent of the women in gay relationships said that they could talk easily and openly with their women lovers. (For a fuller discussion of gender and listening behavior, see Borisoff and Merrill 1991.)

However, it is important to keep in mind that biological sex alone does not determine our interaction strategies any more than it determines absolutely the verbal or vocal behaviors in which we engage. In a fascinating study on the effects of gender on conversation, Kriss Dass (1986) explored same-sex conversations to investigate the use of "dominating" interaction patterns in communication with same sex partners. Unlike sex, which is a biological entity, gender implies a socially learned notion of masculinity or femininity. Women may identify with some traits that are considered masculine; men may identify with some traits considered feminine. In Dass' study, ninety-one students participated in roleplays with same sex partners. The conversations were recorded and analyzed for instances of overlap and interruption. Dass found that *regardless of the subject's sex*, the more male-like her or his internalized gender identity (according to the Burke and Tull gender identity measure), the greater the likelihood that a person will initiate an interruption during a conversation.

Clearly our patterns of speaking, listening and responding to one another are open to various interpretations, are motivated by diverse intentions and may be read in ways which facilitate or disrupt effective communication. As a way of encouraging more collaborative and less hierarchical exchanges, we suggest the following strategies.

1. In every interruption or overlap, there is an interrupter and a person who consents to the interruption. The person being interrupted need not acquiesce. She or he should continue speaking or calmly state, "You interrupted me. I haven't finished speaking yet."

2. When attempting to initiate or develop a topic and receiving only minimal responses, the first member of the dyad might revise his or her questioning strategies by asking increasingly more open questions.

   For example, if the response to "Was the stock merger successful?" is a minimal "Uh huh" the initiator should not ask additional bi-polar (yes-no) questions, or open-ended "How did it go?" questions. Instead, "What aspects of your presentation were most well received?" is more likely to elicit a satisfactory response.

3. Both female and male listeners need to be aware of the verbal and vocal encouragement they provide while someone is speaking. When speakers feel that their listeners are distracted or that attention is being withheld, they should stop their communicative attempt and identify the *disconfirming responses* they are receiving before the interaction continues.

   Evelyn Sieburg and Carl Larson (1971) examined seven types of responses in which one speaker ignored some significant aspect of another speaker's message. Their research did not specifically investigate gender differences but informal observations in our classrooms have led us to note that the following disconfirming behaviors frequently are present in mixed-sex dyads.

   a. *the impervious response*. In the impervious response, the speaker's comment is ignored verbally and nonverbally.

Women often complain that in a meeting, a suggestion that was ignored when they voiced it was later adopted enthusiastically when offered by a male colleague. Women, children, minorities, the aged, the handicapped—all the less powerful segments of our society—find their messages met, all too frequently, with impervious responses. The resultant feeling of being "invisible" is extremely frustrating.

b. *the interrupting response.* As we have discussed above, the interrupting response is also a negation of a speaker's communicative attempt. Sieburg and Larson identify interruptions that are not prefaced by such injections as "I understand, however . . ." as particularly disconfirming.

c. *the irrelevant response.* The irrelevant response occurs when a listener makes a comment totally unrelated to what the other person was just saying. This is one of the ways more powerful members of a dyad or a group attempt to control the selection of topics and to dominate discussions.

d. *the tangential response.* Related to the irrelevant response is the tangential one. In this case, a speaker nominally acknowledges the other speaker's message, but then shifts the conversation in another direction of his or her own choosing. An example of this type of response follows:

Employee: "I'd like to talk with you about my upcoming promotion."
Employer: "Sure, I know you want a raise, but now you'd better concentrate on your current project so that we don't get backlogged."

e. *the impersonal response.* This refers to a generalized, intellectualized response to a speaker's message. An impersonal response may be a categorical assertion, such as the response of the manager in the following exchange:

Union Representative: "I think we should have day-care facilities available on the premises for children of employees."
Manager: "Women want it both ways. You can't be a

good worker and a good mother. Something
has to give.''

f. *the ambiguous response.* In this kind of interaction, the
respondent is intentionally vague and may be misleading the
first speaker. For example:

Worker: "Am I next in line for a supervisory position?"
Manager: "Could be. I'm not really sure how these things
work."

g. *the incongruous response.* In this exchange the verbal and
nonverbal components of the respondent's message appear to
contradict each other:

Client:"Are you upset that I'm late for my appointment?"
Practitioner: (shouting and banging on the desk) "No,
I'm **not** upset."

All of these disconfirming responses disparage and
discourage the communicative attempts of speakers while
fostering and reinforcing a power differential. We know of no
formal study that attempts to examine the greater incidence of
disconfirming responses in either sex, although clearly more
research in the area is needed. Superiors have the power to
"disconfirm" the messages of subordinates. All of us need to
be able to identify and to eliminate these behaviors if we are to
have more harmonious personal and professional interactions.

Suggested Activities

A. Focus on Listening.

Rousseau's quotation, which prefaces this chapter, motivated
Mary Wollstonecraft in 1791 to write her historic *Vindication
of the Rights of Woman* in rebuttal.

Whereas Rousseau enjoined women by "art" or artifice to
render themselves agreeable to men, Wollstonecraft wished:

> . . . to persuade women to endeavor to acquire strength, both
> of mind and body, and to convince them that the *soft
> phrases,* susceptibility of heart, delicacy of sentiment and
> refinement of taste, *are almost synonymous with epithets
> of weakness,* and that those beings who are only the objects

of pity and that kind of love, which has been termed its
sister, *will soon become objects of contempt.*   [emphasis
added]

Mary Wollstonecraft
Introduction to First Edition
A Vindication of the Rights of Woman

Observe individuals who employ the self-trivializing gestures
and speech patterns identified in this chapter as mechanisms
for making themselves agreeable or to gain the approval of their
superiors. Using the following chart, enter the strategies used
and whether their superiors respond in the desired fashion or
dismiss the communication with ''pity'' or, as Wollstonecraft
claims, with ''contempt.''

Speaker	Message Intended	Strategy Employed	Listener	Listener's Reaction

B. Focus on Dyadic Communication.

In pairs, role play an imaginary dialogue between Rousseau and Wollstonecraft or contemporary equivalents like Phyllis Schlafly and Gloria Steinem. Switch roles and attempt to defend the opposite position.

C. Focus on Small Group Communication: Interpersonal

In a small group, with equal numbers of male and female members, discuss a controversial social topic in front of an audience. For the purpose of the exercise, all the male members should employ the traditional feminine strategies [e.g., tag questions, qualifiers, disclaimers, etc.) and the female members should use categorical assertions and other masculine styles. After the discussion, ask the class or seminar group to evaluate the members according to the following criteria:

Agree			**Disagree**	
1	2	3	4	5

Vocal, Verbal and Nonverbal Behavior

1. Member was an effective speaker.
2. Member was an effective listener.
3. Member seemed well prepared.
4. Member seemed authoritative.
5. Member seemed sensitive to communicative behavior of other group members.

D. Focus on Communication: Exercises to Lower Pitch.

To open up and speak from the lower range of your natural pitch, practice by sitting in a chair and placing a book on the floor in front of you. Lean over limply, with your head between your legs, and read aloud into the floor. Tape yourself in this position. You will hear yourself speaking from the bottom reaches of your voice. Try to maintain this while in an upright position.

In order to maintain the lower pitch, place your hand low on your chest while you speak. By focusing your concentration lower in your chest instead of in a constricted throat, you will remind yourself to bring your pitch down.

chapter **3**

Gender and Nonverbal Communication

I practice hiding my anger.
My lips pout, I permit
old men to kiss me. I seem
eager. I offer. I sit
on their committee; I take
notes. I fold my hands. I keep
quiet when they speak
of what they use to keep me
busy, keep me quiet, smiling, out
of trouble. Their eyes mining me
are old. They try to find my danger,
but they cannot see this paper
is overheating, is about
to burst into flames.

—Joan Larkin

Many of the stereotypes about women and men result from the various nonverbal skills and behaviors displayed by each gender. Some theorists, like sociologist Erving Goffman, discuss the display of gender as a learned behavior, an aspect of one's presentation of self. For example, young girls may be consciously taught to "sit like a lady" with legs close together; young boys learn not to cry or express fear. The gender differentiated nonverbal behaviors that may result from this socialization are learned rather than innate behaviors. Nonetheless, many conclude that men "naturally" take up more space than do women or that women are "naturally" more emotional than men.

Other researchers, like La France and Mayo (1978), posit a twofold nature of nonverbal behaviors; *presentational* gestures, postures, expressions etc. which one consciously presents to others and *representational* expressions of an individual's actual inner emotional state. Further, men and women may differ in their ability to perceive and to decode nonverbal messages accurately. This sensitivity to nonverbal messages of others may also be learned and related to a given society's sex role expectations. In this chapter we will explore gender differences and similarities in such nonverbal variables as space, height, touch, facial expressions, and eye contact.

A. Space, or Bigger is Better.

In American culture, space is indicative of power, and individuals who have command over greater amounts of territory have more power. In different cultures, the amount of personal space individuals need may vary. Within most cultures, the closer people feel to each other emotionally, the more they are likely to allow each other to be close in proximity. Thus, the distance between communicators in an interaction may be influenced by gender, culture, power and the degree of intimacy and reciprocity.

Women and lower status persons take up less space than males and higher status persons. In addition, people of lower status cannot control others from entering the space available to them. The boss can enter the worker's space, lean on the employee's desk, or tower over the subordinate. Only with the supervisor's invitation can the subordinate enter into the supervisor's space. In public and in private, in the workplace and in the streets, women constantly experience space encroachment.

Frank Willis (1966) performed studies in which he measured the initial distance set by an approaching person. He established that both sexes approach women more closely than they do men.

When women's space is intruded upon, they are apt to acquiesce to the intrusion—just as they frequently acquiesce to interruptions. Jeanette Silveira's research (1972), indicated that when men and women walked toward each other on the sidewalk, the woman moved out of the man's way in twelve out of nineteen cases. In the animal kingdom and among human beings, subordinates yield space to dominants. In a review of the research studies on nonverbal sex differences in interpersonal distance, Judith Hall (1984) found that females are approached more closely than are males.

Women are taught to take up less space than men. They are taught to sit with their legs together and elbows to their sides and to walk with smaller steps. Men sit and move expansively. While seated, they spread their legs and put their arms on the armrests of chairs. They walk with longer strides. We know that these stereotypical ways of moving are not anatomically based because men in the Orient, for example, sit with their legs as closely together as do Western women. Yet among Americans, men who retreat into as little available space as they can may not be considered masculine, while women who sit, stand and walk with open movements may be regarded as unfeminine.

Females are encouraged to sit and move in ways that exacerbate their spatial limitations. For example, women may sit, poised on the edge of a chair, eagerly leaning forward rather than expanding into all the space available to them. "Feminine" clothes also contribute to a nonverbal image of female weakness. Tight skirts and tight slacks restrict movement. High heels force women to take small steps.

Some theorists contend that the closer interpersonal distances employed by women are a result of women's greater tendencies toward warmth and affiliation, rather than a reflection of status differences. Hall notes that the smallest interpersonal distances are observed between individuals of equal status rather than between dominants violating the space of subordinates. However, if the feeling of emotional closeness or affiliation between individuals is not reciprocal, an undesired intrusion into others' personal space may be considered a gross abuse of authority.

B. Height.

Height is also a nonverbal variable that may be manipulated, thereby either empowering or impeding an individual. We say, "I look up to you" to indicate respect or admiration. "Higher" like "bigger" is often used to mean "better," or "more" (as in "higher class," "high" opinion).

In hierarchies, the individual with greater power frequently is perceived as taller than he or she is. Paul R. Wilson (1968) reported that undergraduates who were asked to estimate the height of a man who was described as any one of five academic ranks increased their estimation of his height when his ascribed status was increased.

Men are generally taller than women. Since we expect taller people to be more powerful, they frequently use their height to their advantage. Traditional female facial expressions of coyness and flirtation may reinforce the height and power differential between the sexes. For example, women frequently tilt their heads to the side and look upward when talking to men. Although the head tilt is a gesture which indicates attentive listening in either sex, women are apt to employ this more frequently in mixed-sex pairs than men, thus reinforcing the notion that in addition to listening, the woman is looking up to the man.

However, tall women have not been encouraged to use their height to their advantage. In fact, tall women are generally made to feel embarrassed about their height. Rather than proudly "walking tall," the larger woman may feel awkward and insecure. In a world in which height equals power and women are not supposed to be powerful, the taller woman may feel that she is an aberration and that she will be unattractive to men who value weakness in a woman over strength. As a result, taller women may attempt to diminish themselves, to slouch and round their shoulders so as to retreat into or occupy as little space as possible.

We must guard against using height to control or to influence. Superiors need not tower over subordinates in the workplace. Tall individuals should be encouraged neither to use their height in an intimidating fashion nor to attempt to diminish themselves by denying their personal power. Power need not be used as power over others.

C. Touch; or Just a Friendly Pat on the Back?

Touch, like physical closeness, may be considered an expression of affection, support or sexual attraction. However, touch may be used to express and maintain an asymmetrical relationship as well as a reciprocal one. For example, as a gesture of comfort, the doctor may touch the patient, but the patient may not initiate contact with the doctor. Similarly, upon entering the elevator, the department head may pat the elevator operator on the back and inquire about the elevator operator's family. However, this apparently "friendly" gesture is not as benign as it appears as long as the elevator operator does not have an equal right to initiate the same pat on the back and elicit similar personal information from the department head.

In 1970 and 1973, Nancy Henley performed observational studies investigating the relationship between touch and socioeconomic status, sex and age. Henley found that higher status persons (individuals of higher socioeconomic status, male and older) touched lower status persons significantly more often. Henley's findings have important implications for both women and men. Individuals of both sexes should guard against using touch to assert authority. We should avoid initiating touch in situations where either the other individual is not desirous of the gesture or where the higher status person would not accept a reciprocal touch.

What about when the gesture *is* reciprocal? Women and men working together must be aware of outsiders possibly misconstruing the sexual implications of touch. In the Mondale-Ferraro campaign for the American presidency, newscasters mentioned a distinction from previous campaigns. Male candidates for president and vice-president traditionally linked inner arms and waved their raised outer arms, Mondale and Ferraro waved outer arms with their inner arms at their sides. They did not touch each other.

In our opinion, it is unfortunate that either the same sex or opposite sex colleagues need to be circumspect with regard to genuine, reciprocal tactile demonstrations of support. However, the sexism and heterosexism in our society impose restrictions on behavior. Until people become accustomed to perceiving women as competent professionals in their own right rather than as potential sexual objects, they will have difficulty imagining a collegial relationship between men and women without sexual implications. Consequently, at present, women and men who work together will continue to be subject to greater scrutiny than same sex pairs.

Within same sex dyads in the United States, women are generally much freer than men to touch one another. Women friends and relatives may walk arm in arm, dance together and hug one another. Touch between heterosexual males is generally more restricted. Outside of the sporting arena, many American men do not feel free to exchange much more than a slap on the back without their behavior being construed as having sexual connotations.

It is important to remember that the notion of "appropriate" touch, like that of "comfortable" interpersonal distance between communicators is largely culturally determined. In some cultures same sex male dyads have a greater latitude of haptic expression with each other. They may commonly hug or kiss each other on both cheeks, for example, while women friends or family members are much more restricted in their socially sanctioned ability to touch one another.

All of us should guard against ethnocentric and heterosexist interpretations of our own and each others' behavior.

D. Facial Expressions, or "How do you feel?"

Women are expected to be highly expressive emotionally. One of the hallmarks of the feminine stereotype is to be facially expressive, so that a woman's face reflects her emotional state. The most common and easily discernible facial expression is the smile.

From childhood, female children are admonished to smile. They are taught to smile not as an expression of their own pleasure but because it is pleasing to others. The smile of appeasement may be submissive behavior. Women are told that they are more attractive when they smile and appear happy. The key word in the previous sentence is "appear." As long as women and other subordinates are concerned with pleasing others, they are not considered threatening to their superiors.

The same may be said of African-Americans and other minorities in America. As long as one *seems* to be satisfied with the position that has been allotted, the hierarchical system is reinforced. Smiles, therefore, can function as genuine or as artificial signs of satisfaction.

In addition to functioning as an expression of pleasure, pleasantness, or a desire for approval, smiling may also reflect the smiler's nervousness. In a number of service occupations, smiling is not preferred behavior, it is required. In Arlie Russel Hochschild's (1983) article "Smile Wars; Counting the Casualties of Emotional Labor," she discussed the emotional labor required of stewardesses. The flight attendant, the waitress and the salesperson often pay a psychological price for their requisite smiles. When a smile is an *expected* part of the job, it becomes a commodity to be given. Women in these and other occupations frequently are required "to give" male patrons or superiors a smile. The constant feigned smile is an expression of duplicity. (And it must be feigned, for obviously no one can be happy all the time.) An individual engaging in this behavior cuts herself off from the expression of her own emotions. The smile becomes a mask, a form of "make up," constructed to gain the approval of one who has power. Subordinates are expected to smile at superiors. When the boss walks into the room, the secretaries are expected to smile and warmly greet him or her.

However, dominant members of a hierarchy are less likely to smile. They withhold verbal and nonverbal expressions of emotions. Instead, they are encouraged to appear neutral, impassive and to disclose as little about themselves as possible. Rather than smiling to gain others' approval, superiors are apt to assume facial expressions which imply that they are judging others.

One such example, according to Gerald I. Nierenberg and Henry H. Calero (1971), is the disapproving attitude conveyed by raised eyebrows, a partially twisted head, and a look of doubt. (According to Webster's Dictionary, the word *supercilious*, comes from Latin meaning disdain or haughtiness as expressed by raising the eyebrows.)

Little difference has been found in the smiling behavior of female and male infants and young children. As females grow up, they smile significantly more frequently than do males. In one particular study, preschool boys' spontaneous facial expressions were found to decrease dramatically from age four to six (Buck, 1977). According to Hall (1984), "this suggests that socialization, pressure or modeling induces boys during this period to reduce expression of emotion via the face" (p. 54). The social pressure to present a "more masculine" face (less smiling), may be operative for boys at this age since they are in school beginning at age five or six.

In the workplace, smiling should not be employed as an expression of a power differential. Women and other subordinates should evaluate the need to engage in overeager smiles for approval or to offer smiles that are expected of them. Men and dominant members of hierarchies should also reevaluate their tendency to equate smiling with compliance due them. They might also allow themselves to engage more openly in genuine, mutual expressions of pleasure and approval.

E. Gaze, or "Are you looking at me?"

Direct eye contact between two individuals may be interpreted in several different ways. Looking directly into another person's eyes can connote an aggressive threat, a sexual invitation, or a desire for honest and open communication.

Several years ago, actor Robert DeNiro portrayed a psychopathic murderer in the film *Taxi Driver*. Posed in front of a mirror, DeNiro glared at his own reflection, taunting an imaginary assailant whom he envisioned to be staring at him. Menacingly, he asked, ". . . You talkin' to me? Who do you think you're talkin' to?" DeNiro's character interpreted a glance as an attempt at dominance. Researchers P. C. Ellsworth, J. M. Carlsmith and A. Henson (1972) tell us that a stare may have this function. Ellsworth, *et al.* have reported studies that relate staring in humans to primate threat displays. For most individuals, a glance which catches another person's eye for several seconds is relatively insignificant. If, however, eye contact is maintained beyond several seconds, a nonverbal power contest may ensue in which the person with less power ultimately averts her or his eyes. In a number of cultures, children are taught that to look adults in the eyes is a sign of disrespect. Submission is indicated by a bowed head and an averted glance. In mixed sex pairs, women are more likely than men to avert their eyes.

However, gaze has been proven to be related to status and power as well as to gender. Hall's (1984) analysis established that "the more dominant individual gazes more while speaking and relatively less while listening; while the less dominant individual gazes more while listening and relatively less while speaking." (p. 73) Further, Ellyson and his colleagues' 1980 study on visual dominance behavior in female dyads found that females who were relatively high in status gazed an equivalent amount while speaking and listening; lower status female subjects gazed significantly more while listening than when speaking.

In her book *Body Politics*, Nancy Henley attempts to differentiate between subordinate attentiveness and dominant staring. Henley (1977) claims that women and other subordinates look at others more but avert their eyes when looked at. Both of these behaviors are indicative of submissiveness.

In any discussion of nonverbal communication, it is important not to interpret behavior in an ethnocentric fashion. Eye contact, like all other nonverbal behavior, has different connotations in different cultural contexts. There are cultures in which direct eye contact between men and women is regarded as a sexual invitation. For individuals from these backgrounds, averting one's eyes in a mixed sex dyad may be a sign of respect, modesty or disinterest rather than inattentiveness or submissiveness. Because of differing expectations and interpretations for behavior, there is the potential for much misunderstanding in mixed sex and intercultural communication exchanges. Women and men need to be able to identify very precisely those behaviors which seem intrusive or inappropriate and their connection with power inequities in specific social contexts.

As we stated above, women are believed to be more facially expressive (Hall 1984; Leathers 1986). In Hall's analyses of studies of expression accuracy, she found that "females were better expressors, that is their expressions were more accurately judged by decoders" (p. 53).

Zuckerman *et al.* (1982) conducted three separate studies which related expression accuracy to measures of masculinity and femininity. The studies revealed that the very concept of femininity implies clear and willing expression of nonverbal cues. Thus, if being expressive is an integral component in that collection of behaviors which a given society defines as markers of "femininity," males may resist both the nonverbal display of expression and attentiveness to others in order to appear more masculine.

As Buck et al. (1979) have noted, people whose faces respond expressively have lower levels of electrothermal response than do people whose faces do not display emotion. Higher electrothermal responses indicate suppressed emotions and have been considered possible contributors to heart disease and other stress-related conditions which are more prevalent in men than women. Thus, men may be paying with their lives for withholding emotional expression (see Borisoff and Merrill, Gender Issues in Listening, 1991).

F. Decoding Nonverbal Messages; or "I see what you mean."

Research findings support the positive correlation between an individual's successful decoding of nonverbal cues and that individual's own expression accuracy in depicting messages nonverbally.

In Judith Hall's (1984) extensive review of studies of nonverbal sex differences, women were found to be significantly better decoders of nonverbal cues than were men. Women were found to be most skilled in decoding facial expressions. Hall based her review on 75 studies of sex differences in nonverbal decoding skills (1978) and fifty subsequent studies (1984) as well as her work with Robert Rosenthal on the design of the PONS (Profile of Nonverbal Sensitivity) Test. Overwhelmingly Hall and her colleagues found females far exceeded males in the ability to ascertain emotions expressed nonverbally.

To what can we attribute this facility? Several different hypotheses have been offered. Rosenthal (1979) hypothesized that women's greater accuracy in decoding facial expressions may be related to the fact that women gaze at other's faces more in interaction and that "one decodes better what one is paying attention to at the moment" (Hall 1984, p. 34). Related to this is the claim that women's experience with young children and their sensitivity as caregivers necessitate their accurate reading of nonverbal messages (Rosenthal *et al.* 1979).

Hall proposed a relationship between the amount of time that women gaze at their conversational partners and women's greater accuracy in decoding facial expressions. She suggested that "women may seek cues of approval or disapproval or cues that indicate how contented others are from moment to moment as part of a general motive to maintain harmonious relationships" (1984, p. 34-35).

Nancy Henley (1973, 1977) offered the "oppression" theory. She posited that women, and others who have less power, must learn to "read" the nonverbal messages of those who have power over them. Thus people who are oppressed have heightened needs to anticipate and to understand other's nonverbal messages. Henley claims that this is the reason for the greater interpersonal sensitivity of women and other less dominant persons.

It appears impossible to provide one definitive explanation for women's greater facility with decoding nonverbal messages. Basically, all of the explanations offered to date fall into two categories: theorists who relate women's greater nonverbal decoding skills to needs which arise out of their subordinate status and theorists who attribute women's nonverbal skills to their greater tendency toward affiliation with others. However, as Hall contends:

> . . . it is . . . difficult to disentangle these two basic
> explanations — dominance and affiliation — because of the
> possibility that women's lower status reduces their ability
> to challenge or threaten anyone, which in turn enables or
> requires them to act warm and nice (1984, p. 84).

In any case, nonverbal factors such as touch, space, height, gaze and facial expressions exert a potent influence on our interactions with others. Although frequently unacknowledged, many of our notions of masculinity and femininity rest on the nonverbal messages we display and those we decode.

We are often unaware of our nonverbal behavior and of how it is being interpreted by others. This can present obstacles in professional as well as personal settings. Certainly one cannot work effectively if being ogled or ignored, leered at or laughed at. We need to monitor our own behavior responsibly, and to provide feedback to others about what we perceive to be their reactions to us.

Suggested Activities

A. Focus on Small Group Communication: Height and Power Differential

In the midst of a conversation in an informal setting with a group of friends or family members, situate yourself at a different height than your companions. If everyone is sitting in chairs, sit on the floor or stand up. Maintain your part of the conversation. Note people's nonverbal reactions to you. How long does it take until someone else in the group is "on your level?"

B. Focus on Intercultural Settings

Have the class divide into groups of 5 to 6 that include men and women in each group. Each group's task is to create a fictional culture with its own nonverbal norms and behaviors for each sex (allow approximately 20 minutes for this process). Once the groups have established their behaviors, one representative from each group "visits" another group and engages in conversation while using all of the nonverbal behaviors that are operative from the fictional culture they have created. The members of the "host" group try to discern the rules, norms, and roles of the visiting culture.

C. Focus on Nonverbal Stereotyping

The professor or group leader brings in several pictures from magazine ads/articles showing women and men in different professional and personal settings. The pictures are taped to the board at the front of the room. Class members are asked to write a brief fictional account about each figure's life. Discussion follows comparing how the group arrived at the fictional lives of the figures in the photos. The extent to which the figures were sex-trait and sex-role stereotyped is also addressed.

D. Focus on Touch

Keep a personal log of all of the touches received during a two-to three-day period. Using the following chart, identify the initiator of the touch, the situation, the appropriateness of the touch, and the status relationship between the initiator and the recipient, the gender of each, and the recipient's reaction.

Initiator of of touch	Situation	Status of vs Recipient	Recipient's Reaction

chapter 4

Women and Men in the Workplace

Traditions and Advances

But, you may say, we asked you to speak about women and fiction—what has that got to do with a room of one's own? I will try to explain. ... All I could do was to offer you an opinion upon one minor point—a woman must have money and a room of her own if she is to write fiction; and that, as you will see, leaves the great problem of the true nature of woman and the true nature of fiction unsolved.

—(Virginia Woolf, 1929)

"A Room of One's Own" is based upon two of Woolf's papers entitled "Women and Fiction" and has become, according to Woolf scholar Mitchell A. Leaska (1984), "the classic essay on feminism" (p. 168). What is striking about the above-cited quotation is its simplicity. For the artist to write, she must have a place to call her own; she must have a roof over her head. In Victorian England, male economic dominance was, in Woolf's view, a major barrier to artistic achievement and the root of many real problems for women. Sadly, many of the barriers to owning one's room persist for American women in the 1990s.

During the past two decades more and more women entered fields that had been almost exclusively the domain of men. A great deal of research has been published on the sociological causes and impact (Bernard, 1981; Blumstein and Schwartz,

1983; Hochschild, 1990; Rubin, 1983, etc.) and on the economic realities (Heilman, 1983; Major, 1987; Morrison et al., 1987; Powell, 1988; Stewart and Ting Toomey, 1987; Wallace, 1982, etc.) that affect equality in the work place.[1]

Many factors have contributed to the barriers women (and to a certain extent, men) face in developing their communication strategies, in pursuing their social relationships, in seeking career goals, and in balancing work and family demands. This chapter examines five major factors that contribute to our gender traits and sex-role identities while simultaneously erecting the walls that keep women longing for a room of their own. We have drawn from diverse fields — management, psychology, sociology, education, communication, the mass media — and have attempted to present these distinct threads cohesively.

Socialization: Growing Up Male and Female

We all share certain expectations about what it means to grow up as a male or female in U.S. culture. Gender-role identity exerts its influence from the moment a baby is born. Sociologist Jesse Bernard (1981) observes that "Is it a boy?" or "Is it a girl?" is more than merely a casual question. From that question develops how the mother, the father, siblings, friends — how society in general — will respond to the newborn. From that question develops the characteristics and roles that will feminize or masculinize the baby.

As social psychologists Williams and Best (1982) have determined, the characteristics assigned to each sex are not limited to U.S. culture. Characteristics assigned on the basis of gender are called sex-trait stereotypes which the researchers define as those "psychological characteristics or behavioral traits

---

[1]We recognize that the body of research cited overwhelmingly assumes heterosexual orientation. We acknowledge that some of the expectations with regard to the conflicting pressures on individuals in relationships, the family, and the work place, will be operative as well for gay, lesbian, and cohabiting heterosexual couples, as reflected in Blumstein and Schwartz (1983). However, some of the issues facing men and women in these populations are sufficiently complex to be beyond the scope of what can be covered in a book of this size.

that are believed to characterize men with much greater (or lesser) frequency than they characterize women" (p. 16). In a pan-cultural study spanning 30 nations, the adjectives "adventurous," "dominant," "forceful," "independent," "masculine," and "strong-willed" were applied to men; terms such as "emotional," "sentimental," "submissive," "nurturing," and "superstitious" were consistently assigned to women.

The above terms taken in isolation have little meaning. However, within the context of culture, they speak volumes about attitudes toward men and women. If a society constructs a paradigm that values especially one set of traits, then the traits omitted may be ignored or trivialized. Scholars from the fields of psychology (Bailyn, 1982; Gilligan, 1982; Harlan, 1982), communication (Berryman-Fink and Eman-Wheeless, 1987; DeWine, 1987; Jablin, Putnam, Roberts and Porter, 1987; Ross and Todd-Mancillas, 1987; Stewart, 1982), and management (Graves and Powell, 1988; Hughes, 1987; Powell, 1988; Wallace, 1982) have all found that corporate culture in the United States developed from a male mode of behavior.

Little boys are encouraged to embrace the traits that will enhance their professional development. If little girls try to embrace the same traits, they usually must deny or repress traits that characterize them as being feminine. It is hard to divest oneself of one's upbringing. As Putnam (1983) argues, women are often trapped when they attempt to adapt to male styles of communication while maintaining some semblance of femininity. In their study on 76 executive women in 25 companies, Morrison and her colleagues (1987) found this conflict between gender roles especially problematic for women trying to make it to the top: "Many of the pioneer women in our study felt terribly confined. They had to avoid being feminine *and* avoid being macho. They had to get the right kinds of help *and* succeed on their own. They had to take risks without making mistakes. They had to keep the home fires burning while they made their career" (p. 145). The men, they found, had only to be men. The women had to be both women and men.

Given the lack of work-role conflict for men and the sustained conflict for women, we would not be surprised to see these conflicts echoed in the professional and personal aspirations of young men and women. When we begin our lectures on gender differences, many of the students at first assert that the differences do not exist any more, that avenues for professional development are available equally to women and men. In part to address the students' assumptions, one of the authors surveyed approximately 150 undergraduate students at a private urban university during 1990-1991. The students were asked to write about how they saw their personal and professional roles in the future. The findings clearly contradicted the students' assumptions, and supported the observation by Alice Kessler Harris, a labor historian, of a backlash in attitudes about women and work in the late 1980s.

The women surveyed were often conflicted about their future. While their short-range goals were clear, their potential roles as housewife and mother were frequently viewed as intrusive dimensions on their goals. One 21-year-old female student stated: "I would like to pursue a career on Wall Street, become very successful, work for about 5-10 years, and then take some time off to raise my children. Ideally, I want my husband to be financially set at this point, so that I don't have to go back to work if I decide that I don't want to." This model of the nuclear family is based on both patriarchal notions of male and female responsibility for financial support vs. nurturance. When they do plan to continue working, as another young woman observes, their money-earning potential is often devalued: "I will always to be a working woman. . . . Hopefully, my husband will be able to provide for me so I can work without any pressure. This means that the money I make will be my own pocket money. . . ." Some young women choose to devalue their own monetary success rather than compete with their spouse: "If my husband is in the same business as I'm in, he would have to be in a higher position than me." Yet a fourth women views her personal life as her top priority: "In my relationship, being a professional will be second to my role as a woman. I believe being a wife, mother, and partner is more important than my profession." The women who were adamant about pursuing their careers often attributed these feelings to the difficulties they saw in their own mother's roles: "I don't want to have to plead with my husband for money the way my mother had to do"; and "The power in my family was with my father—he was the breadwinner; he was the professional. I know I am breaking from tradition, but I don't want to be helpless and totally dependent on my husband."

The unexamined upper-middle class measures of success expressed by these students support power inequities between men and women. Terms like "breadwinner", "pocket money" and "pleading for money", while masking the fact that most American families are dependant on two incomes for survival, reveal the inequities that result from the "provider" "nurturer" dichotomy.

Like the women students, the men also do not escape the powerful social forces that shape our concept of masculine and feminine behavior. One twenty-one-year-old male would like to keep gendered behavior separate: "To me gender differences are a way of life. In the good old days there was a line that could be drawn to separate men and women. That line wasn't supposed to be crossed." He further felt strongly that a woman's role was to be a wife and mother first and foremost. He saw no difficulty assuming the "provider" role and felt that children suffered when mothers continued their careers (he felt, by the way, that women make better parents than men). Moreover, this student acknowledged that his opinion was generally not popular or, at least, not openly so: "If you get the other men to open up honestly, you'll find many of them share my view. They're just afraid to admit it because of the times." Another male acknowledged that women are discriminated against and believed that men do, in fact, hold a privileged place in our society: "Women are discriminated against in every way. Gender differences don't affect me to the point where I will be discriminated against. I'm glad I am a male because we are superior!" A third male had no conflict with his future role as provider: "In a coupled relationship, I, as the male, would feel compelled to be the backbone of the relationship. Backbone would mean being logical, organized, and the eventual breadwinner of the relationship. . . . The woman in this relationship should always be supportive and contribute to the relationship in a democratic manner." Some men, though, did reflect a newer attitude: "Both of us will be working and taking part in organizing a family. I feel that equality is very important in a relationship—to consider your spouse as you would consider yourself."

The messages to these young women and men have not, consequently, changed all that significantly. Largely unexplored are options for men or women not to marry or have children, or to raise children in extended or collective families, or to have fathers alternate as primary caregivers if they choose. As Lillian Rubin (1983) observes, "Whatever the changes in recent years, the message is still: Fathers work, mothers 'mother' even when they also work" (p. 175). The men see their identities tied to their careers—to the world of work. The women, struggling with what sociologist Arlie Hochschild calls "competing urgencies" (cited in Rubin, 1983, p. 160), are trying to reconcile society's expectations to become professionally successful while not ostensibly altering their roles as wives and mothers.

Educational Practices:
A Different Experience for Males and Females

Girls and boys receive different cultural messages about how to behave and about expected roles in the home. These messages, according to numerous studies, are reinforced in the classroom. In the 1970s, much research was conducted that revealed the pervasiveness of sex differences, especially in the elementary classroom. Aileen Nilsen (1977) and her colleagues revealed that the language and examples in children's literature were directed to male audiences. Reinforced in this literature are clear delineations of roles: Boys are supposed to be adventurous, intellectually curious, and to aspire to "important" roles of leadership in society; girls, when present at all, are supposed to be supportive, nurturing, and to aspire to "important" roles in helping professions and in the home.

A recently-published book for young children aims to address some alternative life-styles. *My Dad Takes Care of Me* (Quinlan, 1987) is about a young boy whose father stays home to take care of him while his mother works. On closer inspection, however, the reader discerns many subtle indications about expected behavior from parents, about a woman's worth in the workplace. First, dad is home not by choice but because he lost his job: "The factory closed and my dad lost his job." As a result, "my mom got a new job'' working with computers — often having to ''work at night'', thereby demonstrating the hardship of women who work and who are also parents. Economically, the family has been affected by the change: ''We used to live in a town in the country. We had a house with a big backyard. There was a stream where my dad and I went fishing. After my dad's factory closed, my mom got a new job and we moved to the city. Now we live in an apartment.'' While the young boy likes the city, clearly this shift has contributed greatly to unsettling the status quo. Finally, the reader learns that this situation is only temporary, for dad ''wants to be an accountant. He goes to school now too, only by mail.'' This book tries to deal with the problem of a parent losing a job. No doubt the majority of households are still economically led by the man. Yet educators must be sensitive to the messages even well-intentioned books perpetuate in the minds of the young people who read them.

An article by Laura Shapiro argues that it is *precisely* the issues or concerns confronting males that are dealt with in the educational system. ''[A] glance at the way society treats gender differences already on record is not very encouraging. Boys learn to read more slowly than girls, for instance, and suffer more reading disabilities such as dyslexia, while girls fall behind in math when they get to high school.'' Teachers scurry to get the boys caught up with their reading. Jean Gleason, Boston University professor of psychology, asks ''[W]here are the remedial math teachers? Girls are *supposed* to be less good at math, so that difference is incorporated into the way we live'' (cited in Shapiro, 1990, p. 57). All too often, therefore, the academic needs of young women are ignored because they are an acceptable part of our cultural expectations.

Mothers' and fathers' messages play a significant role in how their children perform mathematically. According to Pedro, Wolleat, Fennema, and Becker (1981), ''Males more than females perceive mathematics as an appropriate activity for males by stereotyping mathematics as a male domain'' (p. 208). Fennema and Sherman (1977) contend that although females have as much mathematics potential as do males, parents have a major influence on female mathematical development. The authors specifically note the importance of fathers and the relationship between the father's general attitudes toward gender roles and their daughter's mathematical development. Recent studies, in fact, support the relationship between a girl's achievement and competency and birth order. First born daughters are encouraged more readily to fulfill their potential regardless of gender-expectations by fathers.

Different gender-based learning styles have important implications for later success. Deborah Brecher, who heads the Women's Computer Literacy Project in San Francisco, maintains that different styles of learning, ". . . especially the emphasis on the role-based games of boyhood, enhance men's adaptiveness to computer experimentation." This difference sustains disparities in the workplace: "to limits on how far women can go in the computer business and to a disappointment of the hopes that this new industry would be free of the sex disparities of older fields of work" (cited in Markoff, 1990, p. 1).

Despite efforts to equalize classroom learning experiences, recent studies indicate that girls and boys and men and women not only receive different education, they learn to expect divergent experiences from the educational process. Myra and David Sadker published the results of a study about how fourth, sixth, and eighth graders receive instruction in mathematics, science, language arts, and English. "At all grade levels," they found, "in all communities and in all subject areas, boys dominated classroom communication. They participated in more interactions than girls did and their participation became greater as the year went on" (1985, p. 56). In reviewing the students' performance, however, what also emerged was that the *teachers* themselves behaved differently toward the males and females in the classroom. Girls were expected to behave politely and were sanctioned when they attempted to call out answers without raising their hands. The boys, in contrast, were not reprimanded for identical behavior. Moreover, they were given consistent, precise, and positive feedback while the girls in the class did not receive the same level of positive reinforcement. The hundreds of teachers, both male and female, observed for this study were frequently unaware of the differential messages they were giving their students.

While young children typically do not have choices about the kind of educational experiences they receive on the primary and secondary level, their experiences at these levels, along with how they have been socialized, clearly influence the choices they make and their expectations for higher education. A three-year study by Harvard Assessment Seminars indicated that "men and women often approach their studies with sharply different values" (Fisk, 1990, p. B8). Men's satisfaction in college correlated positively with their grades. They sought out college advisors who would provide concrete information (for example, "You need to take the following courses in order to get into law school."). According to the study, satisfaction for women is shaped "far more by personal relationships and by informal encounters and meetings with faculty and advisers" (Fiske, 1990, p. B8).

Whether biological or sociological differences contribute to the educational climate should not be an excuse for not addressing these differences, according to Cynthia Fuchs Epstein (1990). She maintains, "it doesn't mean we couldn't do anything about it. People can make from scientific findings whatever they want" (p. 57). It is important, therefore, for educators to acknowledge the conflicting messages males and females receive in the classroom and to realize that sustaining differences in academic performance can affect significantly how each gender will succeed as adults both in the workplace and in their personal relationships.

Entering the Workplace: The Prevalence of Stereotyping

According to Sue DeWine (1987), a corporate culture can be defined as follows: "[A] set of expected behaviors that are generally supported within the group. This set of expectations or norms usually consists of unwritten 'rules' that have an immense impact on behavior within the culture" (p. 19). If a culture has, to this point, been developed and dominated by white men, it follows that male strategies for communicating and behaving would, in essence, define that culture. As Berryman-Fink and Eman-Wheeless (1987) point out, "Organizational norms for effective management behavior have derived from military and team-sports models where objectivity, competitiveness, aggressiveness, risk-taking propensity, teamwork strategies, and chain of command are emphasized'' (p. 91). As more and more women enter and advance in fields traditionally dominated by men, our conception of these norms are apt to change. At this point, however, it is important to acknowledge the impact of unarticulated stereotypes on recruiting, interviewing, hiring, and promoting women in organizations. In addition to stereotypes about gender, women and men are affected by an organization's unarticulated assumptions about race, ethnicity, socioeconomic class, religion and sexual preference. We enter the workplace not only as men and women, but as individuals with membership in multiple identity groups.

In 1986 *The Wall Street Journal* issued a special report on the corporate woman. Although more than a decade has passed since large numbers of American women have entered corporations as first-level managers, most have not advanced through the ranks beyond jobs ''with little authority and relatively low pay'' (Hymowitz and Schellhardt, 1986, p. 10). The authors found that prejudicial corporate traditions, the lack of sponsor advocates within an organization, and the assumption that women's familial responsibilities will take precedence over their career commitments all contributed to the ''Glass Ceiling'' confronted by females in management. However, ''the biggest obstacle women face is also the most intangible: Men at the top feel uncomfortable with women beside them'' (Hymowitz and Schellhardt, 1986, p. 10).

Despite stereotypes to the contrary, a survey by the American Management Association of 1,460 managers found that women did not differ from men significantly in their management styles, women managers were more likely than men to relocate for promotions, and ''in conflicts between important home and business responsibilities, [executive women were] more likely to favor their jobs'' (Hymowitz and Schellhardt, 1986, p. 5d). Nonetheless, the prevalent stereotypes still serve as justification for some to exclude women from managerial positions.

Women managers and executives are more likely to be promoted in industries that hire more women within their ranks such as financial services and retailing than in technology, manufacturing and heavy industry which are even more male-dominated.

However, even in careers as apparently "gender neutral" as teaching, women experience continued job discrimination. On March 18, 1983, federal Judge Lee P. Gagliardi ruled that the City University of New York had "discriminated unlawfully against women on its teaching staff . . . by paying them less than men in equivalent positions" (McFadden, 1983). The ruling affected as many as 10,000 women who taught for the CUNY system from 1968 to 1983. As the plaintiff's attorney Judith Vladeck remarked "What we have sought all along was change, so that in the future there would be no differential treatment of women and men." However, as the current statistics of *Academe*, (the journal of the American Association of University Professors) attest, male professors continue to earn more than their female colleagues.

Aside from executive and academic positions, women are still more likely than men to enter the field of their choice through clerical positions. All too often women remain locked in the "pink collar" ghetto of female-dominated and service occupations. Further, occupations that once were male dominated (teachers, secretaries and bank tellers) have dropped in status and in pay since they became female dominated (Bernard, 1981).

Numerous societies tend to devalue and regard as trivial work that is associated with women. In the Soviet Union medicine and dentistry tend to be female-dominated fields. Those occupations are not regarded there with the social status they receive in the United States.

Whatever the field, women are more likely than men to be evaluated in terms of their physical attributes and age. As the recent books by journalists Linda Ellerbee (1991) and Christine Craft (1986) demonstrated, women who are perceived as traditionally feminine may be devalued as "twinkies," but competent older women who are larger than "model" thin by white American standards frequently find that their employment is more dependent on how they look than is that of their male colleagues. Some occupations, like flight attendants, have won a battle over the age and marital restrictions which were previously imposed on their largely female constituency. However, those occupations may still maintain a weight restriction which is unrelated to the performance of their job.

Studies conducted during the 1980s reveal that from entry to exit, women are typically treated differently than their male colleagues. Even before they enter the workplace, according to McIntyre, Mohberg, and Posner (1980), women experience discrimination. In their study on responses to unsolicited resumes, these researchers found that women were less likely than men to receive responses from companies. A second factor that can predispose recruiters toward one or the other gender is a lack of sufficient information about recruitees. Heilman's (1983) study on sex bias in work settings indicates that when concrete information is lacking, individuals tend to rely on stereotypes. Powell (1988) points to the hazards of such stereotyping. In male-intensive positions (medicine, engineering, military, etc.), men may be regarded more favorably. In such female-intensive positions as nursing, elementary-school teaching, and secretarial work, which are traditionally afforded less status and financial reward the opposite results are evident. Thus, before the candidate arrives in person, gender-role stereotypes in the mind of the interviewer may already have been engaged.

Meeting the applicant does not mitigate the effects of gender. Appearance, according to Heilman, also affects hiring decisions. "Applicants who are judged as attractive have an advantage over other applicants when they are applying for positions seen as appropriate for their own sex" (cited in Powell, 1988, p. 93). (We would caution however, that even the concept of attractiveness is culturally influenced.) However, the objectification of women with regard to their attractiveness may backfire because of stereotyped notions about attractiveness and gendered behavior. That it, women traditionally regarded as "attractive" may be assumed to be "feminine," but the socially constructed concept of of femininity does not coincide with the masculine paradigm of the corporate culture as explained by DeWine, Berryman-Fink and Eman-Wheeless (1987) at the beginning of this section. Thus, individuals may subconsciously anticipate that stereotypically "feminine" women would not perform in managerial or nontraditional careers as well as women who do not conform to the feminine stereotype or as men in positions requiring aggressiveness and competitiveness since these behaviors conflict directly with an understanding of "feminine" behavior as stereotypically more compliant and accommodating.

The culture of every business and organization contains implicit norms for its members' appearance. The dimension of dress is a form of artifactual communication which also influences hiring decisions. Studies by Forsythe, et al. (1985) and Hughes (1987) indicate that women, in particular, will be judged by their dress for interviews. Certainly men are also judged by their appearance. The researchers indicate that white socks, rumpled shirts, too-short ties, and ill-fitted suits, for example, create negative impressions and often result in decisions not to hire inappropriately-attired men. Women who dress for success in more masculine-like dress "received more favorable hiring recommendations than those with more feminine dress. . . ." (Powell, 1988, p. 94). However, dressing in "too masculine" a style could result in negative hiring decisions as a result of sex-role stereotyped or homophobic interpretations of the woman's display of gender. The issue, of course, is not that one should dress inappropriately for an interview. The irony is that men should dress as men—albeit neat and well-fitted. They nevertheless, are expected simply to maintain their role as men. Women, in contrast, are encouraged not to dress in too feminine a manner; perhaps the perception is that such apparel would be too frivolous for the workplace. So they, too, must dress like men—but not so much like men that they risk being evaluated as masculine. Clothing, like language, is a symbol which can be read as a mark of "in-group" belonging, or fitting in. The double bind faced by women in a professional setting then, is how to communicate their "in-group" status as a part of the work team, while acknowledging that they are women. This is further complicated because women are encouraged to construct and display a "style" as if it were reflective of their personality, and for which they will be judged. Thus, the apparently trivial concern with dress is actually an arena wherein individuals communicate the degree to which they want to present themselves or to conform to the workplace.

A final factor affecting hiring decisions is attribution of bias. Despite ethnical and legal constraints organizations may make hiring decisions based on the *perception* that others are uncomfortable dealing with women, men (or any other ethnic or religious group). In 1981, Epstein's study of law firms revealed that frequently women were not hired because the hiring attorneys believed that clients would not be as comfortable dealing with women as they would with men. A recent article on women in business indicates that even when hired, women may find that they are not afforded the opportunity to participate fully. Diana Henrique (1989) explains a male-only party for Japanese visitors: "It was deemed important that the Japanese visitors be put at ease, that they feel at home. And at home is where the women in their lives traditionally stay. So their ever-so-tactful New York hosts apparently decided that their women—wives and executives—should stay home too" (B, 1f).

Graves and Powell's (1988) recent study on hiring practices in business, however, projects a brighter picture for women entering the business world. According to the study, "the applicant's subjectively measured qualifications, such as communication ability, knowledge of the job being applied for, and initiative, had the greatest effect on recruiters' evaluations, whereas applicant sex did not affect these evaluations at all" (p. 95). Although we might question the optimism of these researchers, interviewers are less likely to rely on gender-based stereotypes if they have access to sufficient information about and can meet with prospective employees. Further, bias need not be intentional or conscious to have occured.

Once hired, studies reveal that women do not fare the same as men within organizations. In many organizations and occupations, women earn far less than their male counterparts. A striking work by Brenda Major (1987) examines women's reactions to earning less in comparable positions to men. In a series of studies, she finds that women tend to compare their expectations with other women. If other women earn less than men, this becomes the basis for comparison. Women tend to devalue their own achievements; when they do succeed, they often attribute their success to luck rather than to skill. Finally, Major's research reveals that women differ from men in their career-entry and career-peak salary expectations: "Women felt they deserved less pay for their work than did men" (p. 139). Only by raising women's consciousness about inequities and inequalities in the professional compensation and reward system can women begin to change their own notions of entitlement. In the author's words, "For women to recognize the degree to which they are victimized and undervalued in society and its agents entails psychic costs. So, too however, does blaming oneself rather than the system for failing to obtain desired rewards" (p. 145).

Mobility for women at higher levels within organizations is a final barrier to career satisfaction. Balancing home, childcare and professional life provides a major conflict for many families. Because this issue is so pervasive, cutting across economic, ethnic, career, and educational lines, it is treated separately later in the chapter. However, in spite of the familial conflicts which are indeed considerable, many women in management positions find that there is no road to the top. There are several possible causes for this roadblock. Some are gender-related while others are more likely a result of being in the minority and would, therefore, apply to any token members of an organization.

First, the gender-related causes. As explained in the section on socialization, our culture expects women to be the nurturers and to be better at dealing with relationships than men. Consequently, when morale problems occur, women may be assigned to deal with them. According to Morrison, et al., (1987), this can result in women being overlooked for assignments that could advance their careers. Stewart (1982) concurs. She believes that the task assignments given to women may differ from those given to men, thereby preventing women from engaging in those experiences that could lead to promotion.

A second gender-related barrier to women's upward movement within the organization is that women were not taken as seriously in the workplace as their male colleagues until recently. As more women are recruited into line positions, the "glass ceiling" Morrison and her colleagues describe is beginning to crack.

Women encounter two additional barriers which they share with other minorities in the professional setting. The result, regardless of who is the target, are the same: upward movement is difficult. First, tokens (minority populations) often experience isolation and frustration. For women (or other isolated employees) in fields previously dominated by white men, a lack of role models often makes it difficult to hone the successful strategies that lead to success. Second, because women who reach higher positions tend to be more isolated, as Stewart (1982) cautions, this lack of exposure to other employees impedes the kind of networking that is important for career advancement.

Whether the cause is bias, stereotyping, or lack of exposure, research during the past two decades clearly demonstrates that women in U.S. culture have experienced barriers to the workplace. However, the numbers of women entering male-dominated professions continues to climb. Castro (1990, pp. 50-52) reports that 18 percent of doctors today are women; 22 percent are lawyers; 32 percent are computer systems analysts; and, nearly 50 percent have become accountants and auditors. Researchers agree that as greater number of women and men work together, the professional climate is likely to change.

Redefining the Communication Climate: Uniting Perspectives

> When a woman behaves like a man, why doesn't she behave like a nice man?
>
> —(Edith Evans, 19th century English actress)

Evans' observation of nearly a century ago foreshadowed difficulties many women face when they endeavor to fit in with organizational culture. In recent decades, much research has been conducted on men's and women's styles of communication and on what is regarded as the preferred and appropriate styles for each gender. This section examines some of the changes that have emerged regarding communication within the professional setting and explores some of the myths and realities about leadership styles. (Most studies from diverse fields such as linguistics, communication, or management focus on managerial communication. We will also limit our discussion to managerial contexts.)

Traditional management models favored communication characterized by aggressiveness, objectivity, and competitive-ness. The ability to argue effectively was similarly viewed as a mark of leadership (Rancer and Dierks-Stewart, 1987, p. 18). Persuading another, "winning" a point or a contract, is frequently discussed in terms that favor a conquest/conversion model of discourse. This win/lose notion of management while reflecting an ancient adversarial notion of rhetoric clearly favored men's communication styles in the workplace. Anthropologists Daniel Maltz and Ruth Borker (1982) found several gender differences in the communication styles of women and men. Key to our understanding of the managerial model is that boys learn conversation around competitiveness and dominance while girls learn conversation around affiliation and equality. Thus, the linguistic strategies encouraged in young girls would be regarded more negatively in the workplace (see Gearhart 1979).

As explained in chapters 2 and 3, writers during the 1970s, such as Lakoff (1975), encouraged women to scrutinize their communication styles and to adapt their behavior to the more powerful communication norms—that is, to the male model (based on the hypothesis that women's communication reflected weakness and powerlessness). Translating their experiences into the male code in order to express themselves effectively silenced women's voices. Women became, in Kramarae's words, a muted group (1981). In reviewing the changes in preferred communication styles, Fern Johnson (1983) called this adapt-to-the-male-style model a deficit position. Women were encouraged to abandon communication behaviors identified as weak when employed by women (tag questions, hedges, qualifiers, fillers, compound requests, etc.).

As increased number of collegial relationships developed between women and men, it became evident that some women and men employed similar communication strategies. The differences, it appeared, were in the interpretation of the style and the relative power afforded to the speaker. Bradley (1981) reported that when either gender deviates from expected norms, the communication may be viewed differently. For example, when women use such stereotypical feminine strategies as tag questions or hedges, they are considered unassertive or tentative. Men employing the same tactics are often regarded as polite and other-centered (p. 90). Unfortunately, women may also be negatively sanctioned when they employ men's stereotypical

communication. To speak up and out is to be labelled as strident and aggressive (Putnam, 1983). Men, in contrast, are not criticized for communicating forcefully. Sandra Bem and Daryl Bem (1974) advocated combining masculine and feminine styles of communication. The stereotypical behavior of women and men (nurturing, sensitivity, emotionality, intelligence, assertiveness, independence, for example) belong to neither gender but are, rather, human qualities. The concept of an androgynous model of communication—a blending of masculine and feminine behavior—became the accepted norm. According to Powell (1988), the androgynous model is widely advocated in management circles.

Johnson (1983) identifies code-switching as another strategy for communication. Code-switching refers to employing masculine or feminine styles of communication when situationally appropriate. This last approach has been a staple of second-language teaching. If we accept the assertions of several writers in recent decades (Maltz and Borker, 1982; Reik, 1954; Tannen, 1990) that women's and men's communication shares certain similarities with cross-cultural communication, then code-switching could also be advocated as appropriate for both genders.[2] However, proponents of the cross-cultural model of gender communication fail to acknowledge the social context which affords one code (the masculine) more power. When the two codes are not equally valued, the choice to employ one or the other may further the experience of dominance or powerlessness.

Research indicates that the communication strategies of a good manager and our stereotypical conceptions of a good manager do not necessarily coincide. Rancer and Dierks-Stewart, (1987), for example, considered psychological gender instead of biological gender when studying trait argumentativeness. They found no significant sex differences in trait argumentativeness, yet the perception persists that men are more argumentative than women. Similarly, Harlan and Weiss (1982) studied 100

---

[2] Most of the extant research on professional communication focuses on the androgyny model. Consequently, discussion will be limited to findings on this mode.

managers (50 females; 50 males) from two major companies to determine if gender differences affect managerial career advancement. While they had anticipated finding diversity among the women and men, instead they discovered more psychological similarities than differences: "Men and women were found to have very similar psychological profiles of high power and achievement needs, high self-esteem, and high motivation to manage" (p. 91). It may not surprise us that these stereotypically "male" attributes are found in both male and female managers. It is important that we not confuse cause and effect. Perhaps one may speculate that only those females who exhibit these traits are drawn to, retained and promoted within the managerial ranks, which are still, overwhelmingly male occupations. Ideally, however, Powell (1988) reports that studies continually cite intelligence, nurturance, decisiveness, self-confidence, sociability, tactfulness and initiative as positive managerial qualities. Moreover, these qualities reflect traits associated with both masculine and feminine gender-trait stereotypes.

In spite of similarities in the communication strategies of women and men holding similar positions, the stereotype of the male manager is defined by men and women as preferable in organizations. In a series of studies conducted from the mid-1970s to the mid-1980s, Powell (1988) and his colleagues found that despite their hypothesis that female and male undergraduate and graduate students would prefer a manager with an androgynous mode of behavior, the students consistently described a good manager in masculine terms: [D]espite the increase in female managers and no matter what questionnaire or study design has been used to investigate stereotypes of managers, people have described men as more like good managers than women, and good managers as higher in stereotypically masculine traits than stereotypically feminine traits. Men and women at all career stages examined, including practicing managers, part-time MBA students on the verge of careers as managers, and undergraduate business students, share the same biases about management" (p. 148). Time may mitigate the perceptions that men and women communicate differently in the workplace. As reflected in the studies cited, women and men respond to the *role* of the manager. If that role has been, heretofore, based on a male paradigm, then women and men managers have adapted their communication to fit the role. Only when women and men work side by side for a substantial period of time will the best qualities of both genders in fact alter our conception of the manager. Berryman-Fink and Eman-Wheeless (1987) conclude that as more and more women begin to fill the management slots, "the male-oriented management model is likely to give way to a flexible style that integrates traditional female behaviors and skills with traditional male behaviors" (p. 91). Companies instituting training in listening skills, consensus-building, collaborating techniques, and empathic communication, for example, have already begun to acknowledge the important role stereotypically feminine styles of communication can play in organizational communication.

Home and Family as Priorities: Sharing Responsibilities

> The politics of the family are the politics of a nation. Just as the authoritarian family is the authoritarian state in microcosm, the democratic family is the best training ground for life in a democracy. Those willing to 'strengthen' American families must be willing to strengthen and empower each American — not toward the goal of national supremacy but for reasons of human justice.
>
> —Pogrebin, 1983, p. 18

The Women's Movement has, ostensibly, paved the way for opportunities for women in careers previously dominated by men. Findings from studies conducted at the Massachusetts Institute of Technology, however, qualify women's progress. In white and blue collar positions, in both traditional and non-traditional jobs, "although women are becoming an increasing share of the labor force, they continue to face poorer opportunities than men" (Wallace, 1982, p. xiii). Major obstacles confronting women already in or about to enter the workplace are: Who will take care of the home? Who will raise the children? In nearly all instances, women retain primary responsibility for the home and for child rearing, in addition to their full-time jobs in the workplace (Blau and Ferber, 1986; Blumstein and Schwartz, 1983; Hochchild, 1990; and Stockard and Johnson, 1980). Even when a woman chooses not to have children, these responsibilities can take the form of expectations that she function as caretaker to the other significant members of her extended family, such as her aging parents. Women's familial roles are so deeply embedded in our collective and cultural psyches, the *perception* persists in traditional families that women should retain this responsibility. This section focuses on the following aspects of integrating home and work responsibilities. First, we discuss the pervasiveness of society's expectations regarding women's dual roles. We will then look at the pervasiveness of society's expectations regarding man's primary role as provider and its limiting effects on participating in home-life. Finally, we will report steps some companies are taking to reconcile the work and family conflicts that impinge on the world of work.

The media frequently acknowledge the conflicts facing working mothers: "For working mothers, a quandary when the baby falls ill" is the theme of one article (Lewin, 1991, p. 8). A *New York Times* poll reveals that the *basic* questions facing women that cut across economic and racial lines are: "Who takes care of the children?", "Why do working women *still* do more of the housework?", and, "How do you deal with sexism that is subtle rather than overt?" (Belkin, 1989, p. 26). A third article observes that women's push in to the work force seems to have reached a plateau in part due to our society "that gives women primary responsibility for children yet does not furnish adequate child care" (Uchitelle, 1990, p. A1). One article on women lawyers, in fact, directly connects women's uphill struggle in the profession with their biological clock, concluding that women simply cannot have it all—the demands of the legal profession are too great (Abramson, 1988). Another article reflects the conflict women feel about one another: those who stay at home versus the working mother. Barnton (1990) indicates that one group feels exploited while the other feels ignored and isolated. "The working mom worries her kids will grow up without her. The at-home mom frets she'll never get another job" (p. 68). Perhaps Barbara Ehrenreich and Dierdre

English (1989) best sum up the frustration of professional women:

> We should have seen it coming. For the past 15 years upwardly mobile, managerial women have done everything possible to fit into an often hostile corporate world. They dressed up as nonthreatening corporate clones. They put in 70-hour work weeks; and of course, they postponed childbearing. Thanks in part to their commitment to the work world, the birthrate dropped by 16 percent since 1970. But now many of these women are ready to start families. This should hardly be surprising; after all, 90 percent of American women do become mothers.

> But while corporate women were busily making adjustments and concessions, the larger corporate world was not the "fast track," with its macho camaraderie and toxic work load, it remains the only track to success. As a result, success is indeed usually incompatible with motherhood — as well as with any engaged active form of fatherhood. The corporate culture strongly discourages men from taking parental leave even if offered.

> . . . it is the corporate culture itself that needs to slow down to a human pace" (1989, p. 58).

The issue of child care is also echoed in academic works. In his work on women and men in management, Powell (1988) agrees that "Organizations as a whole do little to accommodate the child care needs of working parents. . . ." (p. 87). Interestingly, he is one of the few to link addressing child care issues to the impact such concerns will have on future generations: "Any actions that organizations take to make it easier for both parents to work will not only affect the parents' decisions to work, but also are likely indirectly to affect later decisions made by their children" (p. 87).

Morrison (1988) and her colleagues found that one of the major factors to derail women on their career paths to the top is integrating life and work. This is especially hard for women, they argue, who must hide or downplay their personal lives so as to avoid negative scrutiny from colleagues and superiors: "For women, it is more important that they visibly limit their family life and personal relationships to convince others that they are committed. The obvious solution for women who want to demonstrate their commitment to the corporation and thereby earn a chance for advancement. . . is to give up everything else, including a family" (p. 114). Thus, what women communicate in the workplace, either explicitly or implicitly challenges or reinforces the stereotypes coworkers, superiors and subordinates have about women's commitment to their work or private life. Additionally, those who try to combine work and family often believe that they can go only so far: "Although both sexes must endure heavy job demands, female executives must serve more as symbols and role models. They also must endure on-the-job pregnancy, the vagaries of child care, and child-rearing, knowing that trying to combine a family and a career might get them deleted from the list for top jobs" (Morrison, et al., 1987, p. 153).

Juggling career and family responsibilities is difficult. Perhaps more disturbing, though, is that this dual role is devalued in our culture. Harlan and Weiss' (1982) study on 100 managers in two major companies reveals that marital and parenting status is unequal in our culture: "For men, marriage and family have been seen as indications of stability and maturity, as well as a sign that traditional values and norms were being upheld. In addition, marriage has proved helpful to many managers' careers because of the roles taken on by their wives. Such roles include providing emotional support, aiding in time management, providing social contacts, and entertaining important organizational members and clients. For women managers, marital and parenting statuses have shown no clear-cut relationship to success" (p. 66). Further, the absence of a support person to perform the "wifely" functions in the lives of women professionals may have a debilitating effect on their careers.

The aforementioned studies and articles signal an alarming situation. Working mothers seem to have little support to help them balance their career and family. The workplace has been largely unreceptive to women's multiple roles, but the workplace is only a microcosm mirroring societal attitudes. These attitudes are rooted in the home. Hochchild's (1990) study of more than 50 families where both parents work revealed that there has been little change in the past two decades in terms of the amount of time husbands contribute to housework and childcare. Women have accepted this "second shift" while trying to negotiate for their partner's increased participation. It is not surprising, however, that men continue to resist engaging in tasks that have been the traditional domain of women; tasks, moreover, that have become culturally devalued: "In a preindustrial setting, a woman's claim to honor was based primarily on her relation to her husband, her children, her home. As the cash economy spread, money has become the dominant symbol of honor and worth. Unpaid work, like that of housewives, came to seem like not 'real' work. The housewife became 'just a housewife,' her work became 'just housework'." Children have ostensibly heeded this message. A 1988 American Council of Education survey of 200,000 freshmen across 400 college campuses reports that *less* than one percent of the women questioned said they want to be full-time homemakers (p. 263).

Sadly, much marital communication breakdowns, distress and dissolution stems from conflict over issues regarding home- and child-care. In instances where both partners are committed fully to work, there is no one to tend the relationship (Blumstein and Schwartz, 1983). When disputes over roles at home arise, the marriage suffers. "In no other kind of marriage was gratitude so scarce, the terms of its exchange so much the object of dispute, and the marital heartbeat so precariously slow" (Hochschild, 1990, p. 127). Small acts, in the words of one divorced mother, could have averted divorce. "If the man would just get up for the night feedings he might not know it at the time—and his wife might not know it either—but that little act could save their marriage fifteen years later" (Hochschild, 1990, p. 273).

In 1973, Young and Wilmott predicted that by the twenty-first century, a more symmetrical family will emerge; a family in which both husband and wife will work outside the home and will share work within the home. "[Then there will be] two demanding jobs for the wife and two for the husband. The symmetry will be complete" (p. 278). Sociologists Jean Stockard and Miriam Johnson (1980) caution that this symmetry cannot occur until attitudes toward caring for home and family are regarded more positively. Happily, many couples in the studies conducted by Blumstein and Schwartz (1983), Hochschild (1990), and Kessler and McRae (1982) make their home and their relationship a priority. These couples suffered the least amount of stress and reported the greatest relationship satisfaction among the subjects.

From what has been written, it appears that most men remain perfectly satisfied with their role as provider; they are content to leave the child-care duties to their spouse, thereby leaving them free to devote themselves totally to their careers. For the majority, this has been the expectation; this has been the role assigned to them by society. It is a role from which they have tremendous ambivalence about trying to extricate themselves. One man articulates this ambivalence:

> I see myself being stripped of my masculine, dominant, father, success image. There it is. I have said it. We were programmed by parents into believing that the male was the breadwinner. His job was top priority. He was to earn, protect and preside over his family. He was the senior partner; she was the junior partner. But the curtain has fallen on those old assumptions, and it's painful and bewildering. So I am afraid for us. Human relationships are delicate affairs. Their circuitry is complex and bewildering. They jam, overload and burn out in the most inexplicable ways. The future is no sure bet. That may be tough, but it is the truth (Fields, 1984, p. 29).

Other men, however, welcome the opportunity to share the household and child care responsibilities. One husband acknowledges his relief about not having to bear the entire burden for supporting a family; he doesn't have "to measure my masculinity by the amount of money I bring in. . . ." Because his wife is with him because she *wants* to be, and not because she is dependent upon him, he values her love even more. "[W]hen she says she loves me . . . I can be sure it's not because she fears she has no other options. In the end, the sense of masculinity a man gets from being loved by an independent woman is more satisfying than a bond forged by dependency" (Edwards, 1990, p. 170). Another man who stayed home for two years to care for his daughter was richly rewarded in unanticipated ways:

> Annie makes me vulnerable to longing, to daydreams, to fears, to pains. She has also made me capable of a love that seems boundless. That lack of constraint sometimes scares

> me. I feel responsible for that love, and wary of its energy,
> but I have grown comfortable with its weight. Annie has,
> finally, by making me a father, made me more of a man"
> (Pogrebin, 1983, p. 130).

For a long time our culture has defended women's primary role in child care because of their biological role in procreation. Yet biological considerations need not be the only criteria for gender roles. Shapiro (1990) argues that "Apart from the fact that women everywhere give birth and care for children, there is surprisingly little evidence to support the notion that their biology makes them kinder, gentler people or even equips them specifically for motherhood" (p. 59). A seminal study by Yale's Kyle Pruett, in fact, supports the contention that fathers who actively participate in raising their children foster healthier gender roles for their sons and daughters. For the past eight years, Pruett has been conducting a longitudinal study on 16 families from diverse socioeconomic backgrounds where the fathers take primary responsibility for child care while the mothers work full time. Looking for subtle but important differences between the children and their peers (the children are between 8 and 10 years of age), Pruett finds that while both sexes evidence masculine and feminine behavior, they were able to play with each other; they didn't separate into boy versus girl play. Most importantly, the little boys knew what to do with a baby. According to Pruett, "they didn't see that as a girl's job, they saw it as a human job. I saw the girls have very active images of the outside world and what their mothers were doing in the workplace—things that become interesting to most girls when they're 8 or 10, but these girls were interested when they were 4 or 5" (cited in Shapiro, 1990, p. 65). Thus, whether consciously, or merely by example, the fathers studied communicated these multiple role possibilities to their children.

Pruett's work augurs well for the potential expanded roles for men. Today, though, men also confront conflicting roles. Men who may want to alter their roles have few outlets through which to do so. There is no "Daddy Track" according to psychologist Edward Zigler (cited in Allis, 1990, p. 81). Allis (1990) reports that the world of work does not necessarily fulfill all of men's needs: They, like many women, want to feel less isolated. "What is so hard for men, is that there is no equivalent to the Women's Movement to help them get in touch with themselves; to unleash the emotions they have been so carefully schooled to hold in" (p. 82). Just as women a couple of decades ago began to scrutinize and reconceptualize their destinies in our culture, so too, do men want to define themselves on their own terms. "Our obligation," according to poet Robert Bly (1990), "and I include in 'our' all the women and men writing about gender—is to describe *masculine* in such a way that it does not exclude the masculine in women, and yet hits a resonant string in the man's heart. No one says there aren't resonating strings in a woman's heart too—but in the man's heart there is a low string that makes his whole chest tremble when the qualities of the masculine are spoken of in the right way" (p. 235). Other writers from the men's movement, such as Warren Farrell (1972), Michael Kimmel (1987), and John Stoltenberg (1990) describe men's communication in ways which challenge the stereotypes of masculinity while encouraging male bonding and supportiveness.

Women and men both, it seems, are starting to acknowledge the limitations societal gender roles have exerted on their lives. They have come to regard child care not as a frill; rather they view it as a necessity. As more and more couples mutually agree on sharing home and parenting responsibilities, it appears that organizations will respond positively. This response has already begun. Such companies as Gannett and MCI, for example, have developed an impressive track record for increasing the numbers of women in top management positions. They have done so by enabling women to balance job and family duties. For example, a woman who turns down a promotion while her child is young is not penalized for the decision (Castro, 1990, p. 52). Between 1982 and 1985, there was a jump from 600 to 2500 companies actively assisting employees with their child care needs (Powell, 1988, p. 193). This assistance comes in many forms: providing alternative work patterns(job sharing, flexitime, part-time work, etc.); parental leaves for either parent; child care support (on-site facilities, consortium day-care facilities, vouchers for day care costs, referral services, etc.). Such programs would enable working women and men to assume caretaking responsibility for any family member who requires their help.

Certainly more aggressive and pervasive steps are required if we are to support women and men's abilities to share fully and equally in balancing work and family. Virginia Woolf (1984) ends her essay, "A Room of One's Own," by pondering the effects that poverty (the situation for women) and that wealth (the situation for men) have on the mind. "[A]nd I thought how unpleasant it is to be locked out; and I thought how it is worse perhaps to be locked in; and, thinking of the safety and prosperity of the one sex and of the poverty and insecurity of the other and of the effect of tradition and of the lack of tradition upon the mind of a writer. I thought at last that it was time to roll up the crumpled skin of the day, with its argument and its impressions and its anger and its laughter, and cast it into the hedge" (p. 188). Perhaps for women as well as for men, we can begin to think not of being locked out or of being locked in but rather of opening doors.

Suggested Activities

1. The professor or group instructor sets up mock job interviews. The men should be asked the following questions:
   a. Do you plan on having a family?;
   b. How will you and your wife manage child-care?;
   c. If your spouse were offered a position that she regarded as a positive opportunity for career growth, would you be willing to relocate?

   Typically, questions regarding marriage and family are asked of women during the job interview. (Even though such questioning is against the law, many students report that interviewers ask for this information either directly or in subtle ways.) It is important for men, too, to consider their roles in the future. The class or discussion group should look at patterns in the men's responses. Both women and men should be encouraged to think about how they plan to spend their personal and professional lives.

2. Before assigning this chapter, ask the students or group participants to write briefly about how they see themselves

in the next five-ten years. The class may then be divided into groups; the participants discuss their responses. The following may be discussed with the entire group.

a. Did the group share goals and attitudes about the future?

b. Were similar goals and attitudes shared by women?; by men?

c. Do the expressed goals reflect gender-role expectations?

3. The class or seminar group should be divided into mixed-sex pairs. Assuming that each couple are married parents who work and earn approximately the same amount of money, the couples should negotiate the delegation of responsibilities and report on the following:

a. How much time do you allocate to taking care of your children?

b. How much time and what type of tasks do you perform in the home?

c. Prepare a chart that depicts a typical work week (Monday through Friday) and how you have assigned and shared duties related to the home and duties related to the children.

4. The class or seminar group should be divided into mixed-sex pairs. The pairs should be further designated into the following four separate categories:

a. Men interview women demonstrating a strong stereotyped bias about a woman's capability to perform the job;

b. Women interview men demonstrating a strong stereotyped bias about a man's capability to perform the job;

c. Men interview women demonstrating the absence of stereotyped values; and

d. Women interview men demonstrating the absence of stereotyped values.

5. The above groups will simulate an interview for a position in management. The position description is as follows:

"Dynamic individual with strong administrative and management skills needed for high-pressure position in a major corporation. Excellent communication skills a must. This high visibility position includes entertaining clients, and some travelling. Room for advancement for the right person. Salary negotiable.''

The rest of the group should evaluate the interviews using the following criteria:

a. Monitor the types of questions asked by the interviewer and interviewee under each of the four categories designated above;

b. Compare the nonverbal and verbal behavior among the four groups; and

c. Examine and evaluate the speaker-listener relationship among the four groups.

chapter **5**

From Dominance to Change

Expanding Human Potential

> May God be praised for woman
> that gives up all her mind
> A man may find in no man
> A friendship of her kind
> that covers all he has brought
> As with her flesh and bone
> Nor quarrels with a thought
> Because it is not her own.
> —William Butler Yeats

According to Eleanor Holmes Norton (1972) in the Report of the New York City Commission on Human Rights:

> Much of the explanation for the entire range of . . . sex inequities can be easily summarized: job discrimination, continuing inequality in admissions to graduate, professional and technical schools, the stamp of "masculinity" on jobs ranging from banker to television repair man—jobs which require no "masculine" trait for performance, the unchanged attitudes of most men; and the still low level of awareness among women of their own problems.

Although there have been decided changes since 1970 when the Commission first issued its report, many barriers to effective egalitarian communication between the sexes still exist. As the 1991 Supreme Court confirmation hearings of Judge Clarence Thomas demonstrate, the workplace is still a different place for women and men. While Professor Anita Hill's charges and testimony of sexual harrassment were heard, broadcast and debated throughout the nation, one issue was made abundantly clear to all. Communicative messages, whether or not they are intentionally harrassing, may mean different things to men and to women. The dominant person in the workplace can, by the verbal remarks he or she makes to subordinates, create a professional climate that is unbiased and accepting or inappropriately sexualized and harrassing. This chapter discusses barriers to change that are implicit in conventional attitudes about women's capabilities, their self-perceptions and how women are perceived by others.

Attitudes About Women's Inherent Capabilities as a Barrier to Change

Traditionally, women in our society have been defined in terms of reproduction and nurturance, while men have been defined in terms of protection and occupation. But the conventional white middle-class image of woman as wife, mother and full-time homemaker and of man as sole breadwinner belies the fact of most contemporary lives. Women are no longer peripheral members of the work force. According to the U.S. Bureau of the Census, more than half of all females in America are working outside the home. Hence, traditional attitudes about women's natural capabilities may form obstacles not only to their achievement, but to their very survival. These attitudes fall into two basic categories; the belief either that 1) women are not inherently *able* to perform tasks as well as men, or that 2) even when able, women *should not* compete with men in the workplace.

The assumption exists that half the human race is constitutionally more fit for work that requires the ability to nurture and serve rather than to plan and initiate. This stereotype has been used to exclude each sex from occupations that are traditionally associated with the other.

Thus, women have frequently been tracked into dead-end, "entry-level" jobs in numerous fields, while males with similar degrees of experience and expertise have been hired for more upwardly mobile tracts. The female college graduate is still more likely to be expected to break into a field as a typist or receptionist than is her male counterpart. *Women's conventional communication strengths have been used against them,* as an excuse for hiring women and keeping them in positions where they are expected to smile, greet and serve others. Males with identical degrees are more likely to be employed in positions where they may learn aspects of a business and proceed through its ranks. The efficient secretary may be promoted to executive secretary, while the beginning salesman whose achievements are recognized may hope to be promoted to a managerial position. Although it is not impossible for women to bypass either clerical channels or to ascend to more substantial positions within an organization, they still have to overcome the burden of traditional sex role expectations.

In recent years, higher and professional education has become available to larger numbers of women. Moreover, it has become socially acceptable for women to pursue an education, and it is more likely to be financially feasible for many to do so. However, women still dominate the helping professions (nursing, elementary school teaching, dental hygiene, etc.) and men still dominate professional specialties regarded as more prestigious (medicine, college teaching, dentistry, etc.). Thus, overcoming the "stamp of masculinity" is an issue for women in many occupations. The stockbroker and the physician are most often males. Women who have broken into these fields are still clustered in relatively less lucrative, less prestigious, and less conventionally masculine specialties.

Women's traditional skills in and associations with the home and the family affect others' perceptions of their abilities. For example, women in real estate are more often employed in residential than in corporate sales. A much larger percentage of female physicians are pediatricians rather than surgeons. In Jill Quadrango's (1976) article assessing medical specialties, she found that many female physicians indicated that their choice of a specialty was influenced by their desire to avoid possible conflicts which they feared might arise if they entered more traditionally male areas.

Even among those who do not assert that women's inherent capabilities are less or different than men's, there are those who believe that women *should not* enter careers that are labelled as traditionally male. Some argue that women don't really "need" to work. When they do, they may be taking a job away from a male who is responsible for the support of an entire family. However, commissioner Eleanor Holmes Norton (1972) set this assumption to rest when she stated that:

> Eight million women heads of families need to join the struggle for women's rights, to take to task that large segment of the population who believe women work for pin money. So do the 84% of mothers who, though living with their husbands, must work to supplement low male wages; so do the one third of working mothers who go to work though they have children under six years of age and no adequate child care facilities.

Overwhelmingly, women (like men) work because they must— because they are solely or partially responsible for their own and their family's sustenance. Many still assume that females should conduct themselves in a stereotypical manner by functioning in a supportive capacity and eschewing occupations which demand more assertive commnnication styles.

At home, working women are still considered to be more responsible for childcare and domestic chores than are their male partners. Hence, women are discouraged from pursuing occupations that demand a considerable commitment of an individual's time and energies. Employers may fear that women will be less responsible to their careers because of their great responsibilities to their families.

However, women who do not have familial constraints are also restricted in the workplace. Some prospective employers and colleagues regard unmarried women with suspicion. They may speculate that the woman is merely looking for a husband and will leave or lessen her commitment to her career should she marry. Furthermore, women who do not communicate in a stereotypical feminine mode reflecting indecision or uncertainty, may threaten men who are unaccustomed to dealing with independent women who appear not to need them.

Self-Perceptions as a Barrier to Change

In addition to how they are perceived by others, men and women's perceptions of themselves may present significant obstacles. Many women have internalized societal values that place a high premium on traits that are conventionally identified as masculine and a low premium on feminine qualities. Women may communicate this negative self-perception in several ways.

1. Women may attempt to disassociate themselves from other women, in order to distance themselves from males' devaluation of them. As Stockard and Johnson (1980) observe:

   One possible response to devaluation is for women to see it as correct on a general level but to insist that "it doesn't apply to me because I'm not like other women." Thus, women who have made it in a man's world often attribute their success to their being better than and fundamentally different from other women. Isolated professional women may feel, "I made it. Why can't the rest of you?"(p. 16).

By accepting that they are special, unique or unlike other women, females may be participating in their own self-denigration and confirming negative stereotypes.

2. Women may fear that their own success will lead others to regard them as less feminine. Matina Horner (1972) measured achievement motivation of college students. Undergraduates were asked to complete a story based on the sentence, "After first-term finals, John(Anne) finds himself(herself) at the top of his(her) medical school class." Over 65% of the females, but under 10% of the males indicated concern about doing well. In their stories about "Anne," female students expressed fears of social rejection as a result of success.

While men are expected to succeed in the workplace, and in fact are encouraged to measure their self-worth in terms of what they have accomplished in the public sphere, a significant proportion of women anticipate that their success will be resented. Thus women who experience *fear* of success are not concerned that they are less capable than men. Rather, the barrier is a result of an awareness that the more capable they are, the more likely they are to be treated negatively. Andrea Dworkin (1976) contends that women learn fear as a function of femininity, and that the fear women experience is isolating, confusing and debilitating. Women fear if they act in an unfeminine manner, they will be isolated, avoided and ignored. Furthermore, women are confused because they are frequently chastised or punished for the very behaviors for which males are rewarded—for speaking loudly and forcefully, for example. Finally, this fear is incremental. Each time a woman violates sex-role stereotyped expectations, she is subject to such negative treatment that she learns to anticipate the sanctions against her, and so she restricts herself. The tenacity with which both men and women adhere to prescribed behavior patterns and role expectations may therefore reflect their fear of the consequences that change would engender. The fear of change has implications for women and men in personal as well as in occupational settings.

Four kinds of barriers to professional mobility predominate. A belief in a lack of *innate* ability to *perform* certain tasks is one rationale used to keep women from entering certain higher status jobs or from advancing out of lowpaying positions.

Social stereotypes of communicative behavior are another means used to justify why women *should* or *should not* pursue certain positions. In this instance, issues of gender role in society rather than capability is employed to maintain the *status quo* in education and business.

The third barrier to change, and the most potent indeed, is one's self-perception. Individuals who fear violating the traditional norms for masculine and feminine behavior have a great deal of difficulty overcoming the labels and effectuating change.

One's personal relationship may present a fourth barrier to change. Men and women who have grown accustomed to a certain lifestyle and relationship pattern which reinforces prescribed roles are not going to relinquish these patterns easily to embrace the unknown.

Effecting Change: Expanding Human Potential

No matter what women and men consciously say or do, part of every message they send and others receive expresses their self-perception and their sense of relative power. How one speaks, moves or listens tells us how that person sees her- or himself. An individual cannot not communicate. The choice to be silent tells us as much about a person as the choice to speak. Gender-based stereotypes are manifested through communicative behaviors.

In the field of speech communication, gender is a variable that has only recently been addressed. Although there is no aspect of the discipline in which gender is not a factor, relatively few texts deal with the ramifications of these differences. Yet, for the prospective therapist or counselor, a study of dyadic communication and interview techniques is incomplete unless one is cognizant of the potential impact of gender differences upon the interview. Similarly, the business person who studies group dynamics needs to be apprised of the possible effects of differing sex-role expectations in the workplace. The hierarchies of small groups, leadership and role taking functions, are all affected by these differences. Future public speakers in law, politics, education or any other field, need to be aware of how their gender may facilitate or impede the reception of their message. The bilingual student and the future teacher of nonnative English speakers must learn to distinguish those linguistic and paralinguistic constructs that are based on specifically male/female usage from those that are not. And all of us, in the most intimate of the interpersonal relationships in our lives, will only be able to share openly and honestly with each other if we are sensitive to the potential power imbalances between us that may be exacerbated by gender-linked communication differences.

In this book, we have introduced you to these differences and discussed their impact in professional settings. While it would be impossible to address adequately every possible aspect of communication in a book of this scope, we have tried to present you with representative examples of contexts in which gender differences affect communication. We have maintained throughout that although the traditional male mode of behavior has been generally considered stronger and more effective, neither masculine nor feminine communicative acts are *inherently* better or worse, stronger or weaker. Rather, it is the *interpretation* that has been placed upon these respective styles that has led people to value one over the other — to reward certain behaviors and punish others. It is that interpretation that we call into question.

The very existence of this book is evidence of the fact that the world is changing. At the National Democratic Convention in July, 1984, Governor Mario Cuomo of New York asserted that his party spoke for "reasonable people who are fighting to preserve our very existence from a macho intransigence" on the part of politicians who refuse to responsibly discuss the possibilities and dangers of nuclear war. By ascribing the threat of nuclear holocaust to a "macho intransigence," Cuomo was equating global militarism with a specifically male model of aggression. To be intransigent is to be unwilling or unable to compromise, to reconcile or to come to an agreement. The stereotypical masculine communicative behaviors such as categorical assertions, interruptions and commands foster intransigent attitudes.

As we have seen in the previous chapter, there is still a pressing need to overcome the barrier of male dominance in the workplace and in the home. Similarly, we need to overcome the fears and negative self-perceptions of those who are less powerful as a result of others' dominance. Instead of perpetuating male and female styles as polar opposites, we have suggested ways that women and men might use effectively the strategies conventionally associated with the opposite sex. In order for these strategies to be adopted, we must remove deprecatory associations for female behavior by expanding traditional views of strength and weakness.

The stereotypically feminine style of discourse is less direct and assertive than the masculine and seeks affirmation and approval. However, it is only when we look at the conventional feminine behavior through a masculine bias that women's strategies appear "weak" or "passive." Psychologist Carol Gilligan (1982) has explained that "When the focus on . . . individual achievement . . . is equated with personal autonomy, concern with relationships appear as a weakness of women rather than as a human strength." Without the accustomed bias,

traditional feminine behaviors may be interpreted as
manifestations of a deeper human strength. As poet Adrienne
Rich has affirmed:

> . . . gentleness is active
> gentleness swabs at the crusted stump
> invents more merciful instruments
> to touch the wound beyond the wound
> does not faint with disgust
> will not be driven off
> keeps bearing witness calmly
> against the predator, the parasite. (1978, p. 63)

We would hope that both men and women might learn, in
Rich's words, to value and to employ "more merciful
instruments" when communicating with others. As we
discussed in Chapter Four, tag questions and qualifying
statements "were perceived as indicators of uncertainty and
nonassertiveness when used women . . . males were able to use
them with virtual impunity" (Bradley, 1981). In fact, the more
"feminine" strategies can be perceived as "tools of politeness
and other-directedness."

Moreover, women who incorporate direct masculine modes
into their communicative style are often more able to effectuate
their needs than are more traditional women.

Thus, we advocate for both sexes an androgynous model in
which traditional masculine and feminine traits are blended. As
Sandra Bern and Darryl J. Bem (1984) state:

> Men and women are no longer to be stereotyped by society's
> definitions. If sensitivity, emotionality and warmth are
> desirable human characteristics, then they are desirable for
> men as well as for women. . . . If independence, assertive-
> ness and serious intellectual commitment are desirable
> human characteristics, then they are desirable for women
> as well as for men. The major prescription of this college
> generation is that each individual should be encouraged to
> discover and fulfill his/her own unique potential and
> identity, unfettered by society's presumptions (p. 104).

We realize that men's and women's communication will not
be valued equally until the social institutions that anoint one

mode over another are changed. We can begin that journey by looking at, by listening to, and by questioning the conventions that have been embraced by both sexes for so long. Only then will we be able to reach out and understand each other.

References Cited

Abramson, J. (1988). For women lawyers an uphill struggle. *New York Times* magazine section.

Aires, E. (1987). Gender and communication. In Philip Shaver and Clyde Hendrick, eds., *Sex and Gender*, 149-76. Newbury Park, CA: Sage Publications, Inc.

———. (1976). Interaction patterns and themes of male, female and mixed groups. *Small Group Behavior*, 7:7-18.

Allis, S. (Fall, 1990). What do men really want? *Time & Women: THe Road Ahead*, 80-82.

Argyle, M., Lalljee, M., and Cook, M. (1968). The effects of visibility on interaction on a dyad. *Human Relations* 21:3-17.

Arliss, L. (1991). *Gender Communication*. Englewood Cliffs, NJ: Prentice-Hall.

Austin, W. (1965). Some social aspects of paralanguage. *Canadian Journal of Linguistics*, 11:31-39.

Bailyn, L. (1982). The Apprenticeship model of organizational careers: a response to changes in relation between work and family. In Phyllis A. Wallace, ed., *Women in the Workplace*, 45-58. Boston: Auburn House.

Barnton, N. (June 4, 1990). Mommy vs. Mommy. *Newsweek*, 64-69.

Beatty, J. (1979). Sex, role and sex role. In Judith Orasanu et al., *Language, Sex and Gender*, 43-49. New York: New York Academy of Sciences.

Belkin, L. (Summer 1989). Bars to equality of sexes seen as eroding, slowly. *The New York Times*, No. 47, 968, A1.

Bem, S., and Bem, D. J. Training the women to know her place: the power of a nonconscious ideology. In *Women's Role in Contemporary Society*.

Berkin, C. R., and Norton, M. B. (eds.). (1979). *Women of America: A History*. Boston: Houghton Mifflin Co.

Bernard, J. (1981). *The Female World*. New York: The Free Press.

Berryman-Fink, C., and Eman Wheeless, V. (1987). Male and female perceptions of women as managers. In Lea P. Stewart and Stella Ting-Toomey, (eds.), *Communication, Gender, and Sex Roles in Diverse Interaction Contexts*, 85-90. Norwood, NJ: Ablex.

Blau, F. D., and Ferber, M. A. (1986). *The Economics of Women, Men, and Work*. Englewood Cliffs, NJ: Prentice-Hall.

Blumstein, P., and Schwartz, P. (1983). *American Couples: Money, Work, Sex*. New York: William Morrow & Co.

Bly, Robert. (1990). *Iron John: A Book About Men*. Reading, MA: Addison-Wesley.

Borisoff, D. and Merrill, L. (1991). Gender Issues and Listening. In D. Borisoff and M. Purdy (eds.), *Listening in Everyday Life: A Personal and Professional Approach*, 59-85. Lanham, MD: University Press of America.

Bradley, P. H. (March 1981). The folk-linguistics of women's speech: an empiral examination. *Communication Monographs*, 48:90.

Brend, R. (1975). "Male-Female Intonation Patterns in American English." In Barrie Thorne and Nancy M. Henley, (eds.), *Language and Sex: Difference and Dominance*. Rowley, MA: Newbury House.

Brown, P., and Levinson, S. (1978). "Universals in Language Usage: Politeness Phenomena." In Esther N. Goody (ed.), *Questions and Politeness: Strategies in Social Interaction*, 56-289. Cambridge: Cambridge University Press.

Castro, J. (Fall 1990). Get set: Here they come. *Time & Women: THe Road Ahead*, 50-52.

Clifton, A. Kay, Gale, Wanda S., McGrath, Diane, and McMillan, Julie. (1977). "Women's Language: Uncertainty or Interpersonal Sensitivity and Emotionality?" *Sex Roles* 3:545-59.

Courtright, J. A., Millar, F. E., and Rogers-Millar, L. E. (1979). Domineeringness and dominance: Replication and expansion. *Communication Monographs*, 46:179-92.

Craft, Christine. (1986). *Christine Craft: An Anchor Woman's Story*. Santa Barbara, CA: Capra Press.

Crouch, I., and Dubois, B. L. (1977). Interpersonal communication in the classroom: Which sex's speech is inferior? *Journal of the Linguistics Association of the Southwest*, 2:129-41.

Crosby, F., and Nyquist. (1977). The female register: An empirical study of the Lakoff's hypotheses. *Language in Society*, 6:313-22.

Cuomo, M. (July 17, 1984). "Transcript of Keynote Address by Cuomo to the Convention." *New York Times*, A16.

deBeauvoir, S. (1952). *The Second Sex*. H.M. Parshley, (trans. and ed.). New York: Bantam Books, Alfred A. Knopf, Inc.

DeWine, S. (August 1987). Female leadership in male dominated organizations. *ACA Bulletin*, 61:19-29

Dindia, K. (1987). The effects of sex of subject and sex of partner on interruptions. *Human Communication Research* 3:345-71.

Duberman, L. (1975). *Gender and Sex in Society*. New York: Praeger Publishers.

Dubois, B. L., and Crouch, I. (1975). The question of tag questions in women's speech: They don't really use more of them, do they? *Language in Society*, 4:289-94.

Duncan, S. and Fiske, D. W. (1977). *Face-to-Face Interaction*. Hillsdale, NJ: Erlbaum.

Dworkin, A. (1976). *Our Blood: Prophesies and Discourses on Sexual Politics*. New York: Perigee Books, G.P. Putnam's Sons.

Eakins, B. W., and Eakins, R. G. (1978). *Sex Differences in Human Communication*. Boston: Houghton Mifflin Co.

Edelsky, C. (1979). Question intonation and sex roles. *Language and Society*, 8:15-32.

Edwards, O. (October 1990). On being a new man. *New Woman*, 168-70.

Ellerbee, Linda. (1991). *Move On: Adventures in the World*. New York: G. P. Putnam's Sons.

Ellsworth, P. C., Carlsmith, J. M., and Henson, A. (1972). The stare as a stimulus to flight in human subjects: A series of field experiments. *Journal of Personality and Social Psychology*, 21:302-11.

Ellyson, S. L., Dovidio, J. F., Corson, R. L., and Vinicur, D. L. (1980). Visual dominance behavior in female dyads: Situational and personality factors. *Social Psychology Quarterly*, 42:328-36.

Epstein, C. F. (1981). *Women in Law*. New York: Basic Books.

Ehrenreich, B. and English, D. (July/August 1989). Blowing the whistle on the mommy track. *Ms.*, 56-58.

Exline, R., Gray, D., and Shuette, D. (1965). Visual behavior in a dyad as affected by interview content and sex of respondent. *Journal of Personality and Social Psychology*, 1:207-209.

Fennema, E., and Sherman, J. (Winter 1977). Sex-related differences in mathematics achievement. *American Educational Research*, Vol. XIV, 1: 51-71.

Fields, H. J. (January 1, 1984). "On-the-job training." *The New York Times* magazine, 29.

Fishman, P. M. (1980). "Conversational Insecurity." In Howard Giles, W. Peter Robinson and Phillip M. Smith (eds.), *Language: Social Psychological Perspectives*, 127-32. New York: Pergamon Press.

Fiske, E. P. (April 11, 1990). "How to learn in colleges: Group study, many tests." *The New York Times*, A1.

Flexner, E. (1968). *Century of Struggle: The Woman's Rights Movement in the United States*. New York: Atheneum.

Forsythe, S., Drake, M. F., and Cox, C. E. (1985). "Influence of applicant's dress on interviewer's selection decisions." *Journal of Applied Psychology*, 70:374-78.

Gearhart, Sally. (1979). "The Womanization of Rhetoric." *Women's Studies International Quarterly*, 2:195-201.

Giles, H., and Marsh, P. (1978-79). "Perceived masculinity, androgyny and accented speech." *Language Sciences*, 1:301-315.

Giles, H., and Powesland, P. F. (1975). *Speech Style and Social Evaluation*. London: Academic Press.

Gilligan, C. (1982). *In a Different Voice: Psychological Theory and Women's Development*. Cambridge, MA: Harvard University Press.

Goffman, E. (1979). *Gender Advertisements*. New York: Harper and Row.

_____. (1977). "The arrangement between the sexes." *Theory and Society*, 4:301-331.

Graves, L. and Powell, G. N. (1988). "An investigation of sex discrimination in recruiters' evaluations of actual applicants." *Journal of Applied Psychology*. Cited in G. N. Powell, *Women and Men in Management*, 1988. Newbury Park, CA: Sage Publications, Inc.

Greif, E. B. (1980). "Sex differences in parent-child conversations." In Cheris Kramarae (ed.), *The Voices and Words of Women and Men*, 253-58. New York: Pergamon Press.

Hall, Judith. (1984). *Nonverbal Sex Differences: Communication Accuracy and Expressive Style*. Baltimore: Johns Hopkins University Press.

Harlan, A. and Weiss, C. L. (1982). "Sex differences in factors affecting managerial career advancement." In Phyllis A. Wallace, (ed.), *Women in the Workplace*, 59-100. Boston, MA: Auburn House.

Hartford, B. S. (1976). "Phonological differences in the English of adolescent Chicanas and Chicanos." In Betty Lou Dubois and Isabel Crouch, (eds.), *The Sociology of the Languages of American Women*, 73-80. San Antonio, TX: Trinity University.

Hawkins, J. L., Weisberg, C. and Ray, D. W. (1980). "Spouse differences in communication style: Preference perception and behavior." *Journal of Marriage and the Family*, 43:585-93.

Henley, N. M. (1977). *Body Politics: Power, Sex, and Nonverbal Communication*. Englewood Cliffs, NJ: Prentice-Hall.

_____. (1973). "Status and sex: Some touching observations." *Bulletin of the Psychonomic Society*, 2:91-93.

Henrique, D. (August 27, 1989). "To American women: Sayonara." *The New York Times*.

Hirschman, L. (December 1973). Female-male differences in conversational interaction. Paper given at the meeting of the Linguistic Society of America, San Diego, California.

Hite, Shere. (1987). *Women and Love: A Cultural Revolution in Progress*. New York: Alfred A. Knopf, Inc.

Hochschild, A. (1990). *The Second Shift*. New York: Avon Books.

_____. (December 1983). "Smile wars: Counting the casualties of emotional labor." *Mother Jones*, 35-42.

Horner, M. (1972). "Toward an understanding of achievement related conflicts in women." *Journal of Social Issues*, 28:157-75.

Hughes, K. A. (September 1, 1987). "Businesswomen's broader latitude in dress codes goes just so far: Male executives also suffer for their sartorial mistakes." *Wall Street Journal*, 33.

Hymowitz, and Schellhardt. (April 24, 1986). *Wall Street Journal* article, p. 1, sec. 4.

Jablin, F. D., Putnam, L. L., Roberts, K. H. and Porter, L. W., (eds.). (1987). *Handbook in Organizational Communication: An Interdisciplinary Perspective*. Newbury Park, CA: Sage Publications, Inc.

Johnson, F. L. (1983). "Political and pedagogical implications of attitudes toward women's language." *Communication Quarterly*, 31:133-38.

Johnson, J. L. (1980). "Questions and role responsibility in four professional meetings." *Anthropological Linguistics*, 22:66-76.

Keller, E. F. (September-October 1983). "Feminism as an analytic tool for the study of science." *Academe*. Bulletin of the American Association of University Professors.

Kenkel, W. F. (1963). "Observational studies of husband-wife interaction in family decision-making." In Marvin Sussman, (ed.), *Sourcebook in Marriage and the Family*, 144-56. Boston: Houghton Mifflin. Kenneth, C. W. (1980). "Patterns of verbal interruption among women and men in groups." Paper presented at the Third Annual Conference on Communication, Language, and Gender. Lawrence, Kansas.

Kennedy, C. W., and Camden, C. T. (1983). "A new look at interruptions." *Western Journal of Speech Communication*, 43:45-48.

Keohane, N. O. (1981). "Speaking from silence: Women and the science of politics." In Elizabeth Langland and Walter Grove (eds.), *A Feminist Perspective in the Academy*. Chicago: University of Chicago Press.

Kessler, R. C. and McRae, J., Jr. (April 1982). "The effect of wives' employment on the mental health of married men and women." *Journal of Health and Social Behavior*, 47:216-27.

Kessler-Harris, A. (1982). *Out to Work: A History of Wage Earning Women in the United States*. New York: Oxford.

Kimmel, Michael. (1987). *Changing Men: New Directions in Research on Men and Masculinity*. Newburg, CA: Sage Publications, Inc.

Kramer, C. (1974). "Stereotypes of women's speech: The word from cartoons." *Journal of Popular Culture*, 8:624-30.

Kramarae, C. (1981). *Women and Men Speaking*. Rowley, MA: Newbury House.

LaFrance, M. and Mayo, C. (1978). *Moving Bodies: Nonverbal Communication in Social Relationships*. Monterey, CA: Brooks/Cole.

Labov, W. (1972). *Sociolinguistic Patterns*. Philadelphia: University of Pennsylvania Press.

Ladd, R. D. (1980). *The Structure of Intonation Meaning: Evidence from English*. Bloomington: The University of Indiana Press.

Lakoff, R. (1985). *Language and Woman's Place*. New York: Harper & Row.

Larkin, J. (1975). *Housework*. New York: Out and Out Books.

Leaska, M. A., (ed.). (1984). *The Virginia Woolf Reader*. Orlando, FL: Harcourt, Brace, Jovanovich.

Leathers, D. (1986). *Successful Nonverbal Communication*. New York: Macmillan.

Leet-Pellegrini, H. M. (1980). "Conversational dominance as a function of gender and expertise." In Howard Giles, W. Peter Robinson, and Phillip M. Smith (eds.), *Language: Social Psychological Perspectives*, 97-104. New York: Pergamon Press.

Levine, L., and Crockett, Jr., H. J. (1979). "Modal and modish pronunciation: Some sex differences in speech." In William C. McCormack and Stephen A. Wurm, (eds.), *Language and Society: Anthropological Issues*, 207-20. The Hague: Mouton.

Lewin, T. (March 2, 1991). Child care in conflict with job. *The New York Times*, 8.

McConnell-Ginet, S. (1983). "Intonation in a man's world." Throne, et al. (eds.), *Language, Gender and Society*, 69-88. Rowley, MA: Newbury House.

McFadden, R. D. (April 19, 1983). U.S. Court Rules Against City University in Sex-Bias Suit. *The New York Times*.

McIntyre, S., Mohbert D. J. and Posner, B. Z. (1980). "Preferential treatment in preselection decisions according to sex and race." *Academy of Management Journal*, 23:738-49.

Major, B. (1987). "Gender, justice, and the psychology of entitlement." In Phillip Shaver and Clyde Hendrick, (eds.), *Sex and Gender*. Newbury Park, CA: Sage Publications, Inc.

Maltz, D. and Borker, R. (1982). "A cultural approach to male-female miscommunications." In J. J. Gumperz, (ed.), *Language and Social Identity*, 196-216. England: Cambridge University Press.

Markoff, J. (February 13, 1989). "Computing in America: A masculine mystique." *The New York Times*, 1.

Marlatt, G. A. (1970). "A comparison of vicarious and direct reinforcement control of verbal behavior in an interview setting." *Journal of Personality and Social Psychology*, 16:695-703.

Martin. W. (ed.). (1972). *American Sisterhood: Writings of the Feminist Movement from Colonial Times to the Present*. New York: Harper & Row.

Mattingly, I. (1966). "Speaker variation and vocal tract size." Paper presented at the Acoustical Society of America. Abstract in *Journal of Acoustical Society of America*, 39:1219.

Mead, M. (1963). *Sex and Temperament in Three Primitive Societies*. New York: Morrow

Milroy, L. (1980). *Language and Social Networks*. Baltimore, MD: University Park Press.

Montgomery, B. and Norton, R. W. (1981). "Sex differences and similarities in communicator style." *Communication Monographs*, 48:121-32.

Morrison, A. M., White, R. P., Van Velsor, E. and The Center for Creative Leadership. (1987). *Breaking the Glass Ceiling: Can Women Reach the Top of America's Largest Corporations?* Reading, MA: Addison-Wesley Publication Co., Inc.

Newcomb, N. and Arnkoff, D. B. (1979). "Effects of speech style and sex of speaker on person perception." *Journal of Personality and Social Psychology*, 37:1293-1303.

Nichols, P. C. (1980). "Women in their speech communities." In Sally McConnell-Ginet, et al., (eds.), *Women and Language in Literature and Society*, 140-49. New York: Praeger.

Nierenberg, G. I. and Calero, H. H. (1971). *How to Read a Person Like a Book*. New York: Hawthorne.

Nilsen, A. P., Bosmajian, H., Gershuny, H. L. and Stanley, J. P. (1977). *Sexism and Language*. Urbana, IL: National Council of Teachers of English.

Norton, E. H. (1970). "Women's Role in Contemporary Society. The Report of the New York City Commission on Human Rights." (1972, Avon Books).

O'Barr, W. M. and Bowman, K. A. (1980). "Women's language or Powerless language?" In Sally McConnell-Ginet, et al., (eds.), *Women and Language in Literature and Society*, 93-110. New York: Praeger.

Ong, W. (1979). "Review of Brian Vickes' Classical Rhetoric in English Poetry." Published in *College English* (February 1972).

Pedro, J. D., Wolleat, P., Fennema, E. and Becker, A. D. (Summer 1981). "Election of high school mathematics by females and males: Attributions and attitudes." *American Educational Research*, 18:207-18.

Pilotta, J. L. (ed.). (1983). *Women in Organizations: Barriers and Breakthroughs*. Prospect Heights, IL: Waveland Press.

Pogrebin, L.C. (1983). *Family Politics: Love and Power on an Intimate Frontier*. New York: McGraw-Hill.

Powell, G. N. (1988). *Women and Men in Management*. Newbury Park, CA: Sage Publications, Inc.

Putnam, L. L. (1983). "Lady you're trapped: Breaking out of conflict cycles." In J. J. Pilotta, (ed.), *Women in Organizations: Barriers and Breakthroughs*. Prospect Heights, IL: Waveland Press.

Quadrango, J. (1976). "Occupational sex-typing and internal labor market distributions: An assessment of medical specialties." *Social Problems*, 23:442-53.

Quinlan, P. (1987). *My Dad Takes Care of Me*. Toronto: Annick Press.

Rancer, A. S. and Dierks-Stewart, J. J. (1987). "Biological and psychological gender differences in trait argumentativeness." In Lea P. Stewart and Stella Ting-Toomey, (eds.), *Communication, Gender and Sex Roles in Diverse Interaction Settings*, 18-30. Norwood, NJ: Ablex.

Reik, T. (1954). "Men and women speak different languages." *Psychoanalysis*, 2:3-15.

Ryan, M.P. (1975). *Womenhood in America*. New York: Franklin Watts.

Rich, A. (1979). *On Lies, Secrets and Silence: Selected Prose 1966-1978*. New York: W.W. Norton & Co.

————. (1978). "Natural Resources" in *The Dream of a Common Language, Poems 1974-1977*. New York: W.W. Norton & Co.

Rosenthal, R. and DePaulo, B. (1979). "Sex differences in accommodation in nonverbal communication." In R. Rosenthal (ed.), *Skill in Nonverbal Communication: Individual Differences*. Cambridge: Oelgeschlager, Gunn and Hain.

Rosenthal, R., Hall, J., DiMatteo, M. R., Rogers, R. S. and Archer, D. (1979). *Sensitivity to Nonverbal Communication: The PONS Test*. Baltimore, MD: Johns Hopkins University Press.

Rossi, A. M. and Todd-Mancillas, W. R. (1987). "Male/female differences in managing conflicts." In Lea P. Stewart and Stella Ting-Toomey, (eds.), *Communication, Gender and Sex Roles in Diverse Interaction Settings*. 96-104. Norwood, NJ: Ablex.

Rubin, L. B. (1983). *Intimate Strangers*. New York: Harper & Row.

Ruether, R. (1981). "Feminist critique in religious studies." In Elizabeth Langland and Walter Grove (eds.), *A Feminist Perspective in the Academy*. Chicago: University of Chicago Press.

Ryan, M. P. (1975). *Womanhood in America*. New York: Franklin Watts.

Sachs, J., Liberman, P. and Erickson, D. (1973). "Anatomical and cultural determinants of male and female speech." In Roger W. Shuy and Ralph W. Fasold (eds.), *Language Attitudes: Current Trends and Prospects*. Washington, DC: Georgetown University Press.

Sadker, M. and Sadker, D. (March 1985). "Sexism in the schoolroom of the '80s." *Psychology Today*, 54-57.

Shapiro, L. (May 28, 1990). "Guns and dolls: Nature or nurturance?" *Newsweek*, 56-65.

Shuy, R. W., Wolfram, W. A. and Riley, W. K. (1967). "Linguistic Correlates of a Social Stratification in Detroit Speech." Final Report, Project 6-1347. Washington, DC: Office of Education.

Sieburg, E. and Larson, C. (1971). "Dimensions of interpersonal response." Paper presented to the International Communication Association, Phoenix, Arizona.

Silveira, J. (February 1972). "Thoughts on the politics of touch." *Women's Press*, 1:13.

Spender, D. (1980). *Man-made Language*. London: Routledge & Kegan Paul.

Steckler, N. A. and Cooper, W. E. (1980). "Sex differences in color naming of unisex apparel." *Anthropological Linguistics*, 22:373-81.

Steinem, G. (1983). *Outrageous Acts and Everyday Rebellions*. New York: Holt, Rinehart and Winston.

Stewart, L. P. (1982). "Women in management: Implications for communication researchers." Paper presented at the Eastern Communication Association, Hartford, Connecticut.

Stockard, J. and Johnson, M. M. (1980). *Sex Roles: Sex Inequality and Sex Role Development*. Englewood Cliffs, NJ: Prentice-Hall.

Stoltenberg, John. (1990). *Refusing to be a Man: Essays on Sex and Justice*. New York: Penguin, Meridian.

Stone, J. and Bachner, J. (1977). *Speaking Up: A Book for Every Woman Who Wants to Speak Effectively*. New York: McGraw-Hill.

Strodtbeck, F., James, R. M. and Hawkins, C. (1957). "Social status in jury deliberations." *American Sociological Review*, 22:718.

Strodtbeck, F. and Mann, R. D. (1956). "Sex role differentiation in jury deliberations." *Sociometry*, 19:3-11.

Swacker, M. (1976). "Women's behavior at learned and professional conferences." In Dubois and Crouch, (eds.), *The Sociology of the Language of American Women*, 155-60. San Antonio, TX: Trinity University.

Terango, L. (1966). "Pitch and duration characteristics of the oral reading of males on a masculinity-femininity dimension." *Journal of Speech and Hearing Research*, 9:580-90.

Thorne, B. and Henley, N. M. (eds.). (1975). *Language and Sex: Differences and Dominance*. Rowley, MA: Newbury House.

Trudgill, P . (1975). "Sex, covert prestige and linguistic change in the urban British English of Norwich." In Thorne and Henley (eds.).

Uchitelle, L. (November 24, 1990). "Women's push into work force seems to have reached plateau." *The New York Times*, A1.

Uris, D. (1975). *A Woman's Voice: A Handbook to Successful Private and Public Speaking*. New York: Barnes & Noble Books.

U.S. Bureau of the Census, Current Populations Reports series, P-20 (1981, 1982) and series P.23 (1981, 1982).

Wallace, P.A. (ed.). (1982). *Women in the Workplace*. Boston: Auburn House Publication Co.

West, C. and Zimmerman, D. H. (1983). "Small insults: A study of interruptions in cross-sex conversations between unacquainted persons." In Thorne, et al. (eds.), *Gender, Language and Society*. Rowley, MA: Newbury House.

Williams, J. E. and Best, D. L. (1982). *Measuring Sex Stereotypes: A Thirty Nation Study*. Beverly Hills, CA: Sage Publications, Inc.

Willis, F. (1966). "Initial speaking distance as a function of the speaker's relationship." *Psychonomic Science*, 5:221-22.

Willis, F. M. and Williams, S. J. (1976). "Simultaneous talking in conversations and sex of speakers." *Perceptual and Motor Skills*, 43:1067-70.

Wilson, P.R. (1968). "Perceptual distortion of height as a function of ascribed academic status." *Journal of Social Psychology*, 74:97-192.

Wolfram, W. (1969). *A Sociolinguistic Description of Detroit Negro Speech*. Washington, DC: Center for Applied Linguistics.

Woolf, Virginia (1929). "A Room of One's Own." In Mitchell A. Leaska, (ed.), *The Virginia Woolf Reader*, 168-88. Orlando, FL: Harcourt, Brace, Jovanovich, 1984.

Young, M. and Willmott, P . (1973). *The Symmetrical Family*. New York: Pantheon.

Zimmerman, D. and West, C. (1975). "Sex Roles, Interruptions, and Silences in Conversation." In Thorne, et al. (eds.), *Language and Sex: Difference and Dominance*. Rowley, MA: Newbury House.

Zuckerman, M., DeFrank, R. S., Spiegel, N. H. and Larrance, D. T. (1982). "Masculinity-femininity and the encoding of nonverbal cues." *Journal of Personality and Social Psychology*, 42:548-56.

About the Authors

Deborah Borisoff, Ph.D. is Associate Professor and Director of Speech Communication at New York University. She is co-author or co-editor of five books that deal with gender and communication, conflict management, listening, and employing sociodrama to teach communication. Other publications and presentations at national and international conferences include intercultural communication and communication in organizational settings. Dr. Borisoff serves as an active trainer and consultant to government agencies, Fortune 500 companies and individuals in the areas of listening, presentation skills, media training, conflict resolution, and intercultural communication.

Lisa Merrill, Ph.D., is Associate Professor in the Speech Department at Hofstra University. Dr. Merrill's publications and research focus on gender and intercultural communication issues in performance studies, psychotherapy, law, pedagogy, and business. She has lectured widely in India, Egypt, and Ireland. Dr. Merrill is also a registered drama therapist (R.D.T.) in private practice in New York City. She specializes in issues of communication, presentation skills and performance anxieties. As an independent consultant, Dr. Merrill leads workshops on cultural diversity, teambuilding and gender issues in the workplace.